# INTRODUCTION TO BUSINESS ORGANIZATIONS

By Diane M. Baldwin, Esq.
Frances B. Whiteside

Second Edition
© 1999

Pearson Publications Company
Dallas, Texas

ISBN: 0-929563-52-2

# TABLE OF CONTENTS

# ACKNOWLEDGMENTS

Since the first edition of this book was published in 1995, significant changes have taken place in the world of business.

- The terms "home-based business" and "telecommuting" have become commonplace.

- The Internet has made stunning amounts of information available to anyone able to operate a computer.

- Limited liability company statutes have been created in every state.

- The Internal Revenue Code has been amended to provide, among other things, changes in Subchapter S provisions for small corporations.

Two things have not changed, and probably never will: contracts and collections. While this volume can stand alone, combining it with the authors' *Introduction to Contracts* and Barbara Kirby's *Red and Black* will give the reader a firm grounding in the basic principles of business law.

All three books are published by Pearson Publications Company of Dallas, Texas. We thank Enika Schulze and her team at Pearson Publications for their unflagging good humor and support.

Thanks also go to our paralegal students at Texas Wesleyan University in Fort Worth, El Centro College in Dallas, and Southeastern Paralegal Institute in Dallas. They gave us the most practical feedback possible to improve our books with each edition and make them more practical and useful.

Special thanks to attorney and mediator Linda Byars Swindling of Carrollton, Texas, for her generous permission to use the redacted shareholders' agreement found in the appendices.

Diane M. Baldwin, Esq.                                   Frances Beall Whiteside

# STUDYING THE LAW OF BUSINESS ORGANIZATIONS

Why study the law of business organizations? Because you need it!

No one lives in today's society without encountering business and commerce. Whether it's bartering with your siblings, doing business with the local store, trading items at recess, paying the bills, or managing an international company – everybody's doing business.

This book was written with two presumptions:

1.      Simple is better than complicated.

2.      The authors cannot cite statutes from every state in the union.

Simplicity we offer. You, the reader, should keep the specific statutes of your state close at hand.

We will refer to our companion book, *Introduction to Contracts*, published by Pearson Publications Company. We will not repeat ourselves. If we already wrote about the subject in *Introduction to Contracts*, we will refer you to that book.

We expect the readers of this book to be nonlawyers – paralegal or business law students, entrepreneurs, or owners of small businesses. We assume you want to learn about the various ways to do business without going to law school. At the same time, we strongly recommend retaining a good attorney and a good accountant to help you succeed in business.

First, locate the statutes you will need.

## Getting Ready

1.      Where are the acts governing partnerships located in your state's statutes? Find the precise names and citations. Expect to find one for general partnerships and one for limited partnerships.

2.      Does your state provide for a partnership's adopting a status called "registered limited liability partnership"? If so, what is the authorizing statute?

3.      Where is the act governing for-profit business corporations located in your state's statutes? Find the precise citation. Does it mention close corporations?

4.      Where is the act governing nonprofit corporations located in your state's statutes? Is there an act governing unincorporated nonprofit organizations or associations?

5.      Does your state provide for corporations organized by persons offering professional services? If so, determine the name of the act and where it is found in your state's statutes.

6.      Does your state have a statute providing for limited liability companies and professional limited liability companies? Locate its name and citation.

7.      Where is the act governing assumed business names located in your state's statutes? "Assumed business names" are also called "fictitious business names." You may have heard of a "d/b/a" – "doing business as."

8.      Where is the act governing associations found in your state's statutes? What sort of entities are covered by this act – professional associations? Cooperative associations? Other associations?

9.      Some states have a statute called the "Miscellaneous Corporation Law" or a similar title. Is this true in your state? If so, locate the statute and note its precise title.

10. Does your state publish a book called a filing guide or some similar name? For example, every two years the Texas Secretary of State publishes a new volume as the legislature amends the laws. The current title of this excellent guide is the *Filing Guide for Business Organizations and Non-Profit Corporations.* Determine if your state publishes such a guide.

11. What is the universal resource locator (URL) of your secretary of state? Of your state's taxing authority? Of your state's corporate statutes?

---

# Chapter One

# THE BASIC CONCEPT
# OF AGENCY

---

## Principals and Agents

The underlying basic principle behind all business organizations is **agency**. Agency law is simple in theory but often difficult in application.

Agency is a relationship between two or more parties in which one party agrees to act on behalf of the other and be subject to the control of the other.

The participants in this relationship are called the **agent** and the **principal**.

The agent is the party who acts on behalf of the principal and can bind the principal by his, her, or its acts. (Yes, " it" – the agent might be a business entity rather than a natural person.)

The principal is the party who controls the agent and on whose behalf the agent acts.

The agent may be subject to the control of one or more principals, and the principal may have more than one agent subject to his, her, or its control.

This control is usually tempered with a certain amount of discretion that the principal allows the agent to exercise in the performance of the agent's duties.

## Agency Relationships

Agency relationships are very common. Some examples involving natural persons are

- employer/employee

- client/attorney
- homeowner/realtor.

Some examples involve business entities, including

- corporation/officer
- partnership/general partner
- limited liability company/manager.

The qualifications to be a principal or agent are quite simple. The principal must possess **legal capacity**, meaning the capacity to form a binding contractual relationship. If a natural person, the principal must be a mentally competent adult.

An agent, on the other hand, need not be an adult. A child may be an agent even though he or she is a minor – for example, a young person with a paper route or one who runs errands. A mentally incompetent person who possesses a minimal degree of capacity can serve as an agent even though he or she could not enter into a contract on his or her own behalf.

An agency relationship may be created by

- the acts or agreement of the parties or
- by operation of law.

Examples of agencies created by operation of law are those created by statute or estoppel. Statutory agencies are created by a specific statute. For instance, the Oklahoma General Corporation Act appoints the Oklahoma Secretary of State as registered agent for foreign corporations that transact business in Oklahoma. Other states specify the secretary of state as a default registered agent if the original agent has resigned and not been replaced.

An agency created by estoppel is virtually the same as one created by apparent authority, which is discussed in Chapter Two. Estoppel prevents a principal from denying the existence of an agency relationship that, based on the principal's actions or failure to act, another person believes to exist. Silence, or failure to deny the relationship, is an example of failure to act.

Although agency authority frequently arises from a written agreement between the principal and agent, it is not generally necessary to have a written agreement to create an agency relationship. For example, an employee may or may not have a written employment agreement, but it is presumed that an employee agrees to act on behalf of the employer and be subject to the employer's control for certain purposes pertaining the employment.

## Statute of Frauds

When agency relationships are not reduced to writing, disputes regarding the scope of the agency often arise.

The **Statute of Frauds** may apply and require that the agreement between the agent and the principal be reduced to writing. For more discussion on the Statute of Frauds, see the authors' *Introduction to Contracts*.

Briefly, the Statute of Frauds requires certain matters to be put in writing in order to be enforceable. A written document helps prevent fraud that could occur if the party attempting to enforce the agreement was unable to prove the existence and terms of the agreement on the basis of oral testimony.

If the agreement concerns a matter that cannot be performed or completed within one year, the Statute of Frauds mandates that the terms of the agreement be in writing. Thus, an agreement to act as an agent on a matter that will conclude within a year would not be required to be in writing, while a three-year agency agreement would.

Other common types of agreements that may be subject to the Statute of Frauds in your state are contracts for the sale of real estate, leases for real estate for a term longer than one year, and contracts in which the value of the subject of the contract exceeds five hundred dollars.

**The Fiduciary Relationship**

One of the most important consequences of the creation of the agency relationship is the simultaneous creation of a **fiduciary relationship** between the agent and the principal.

The term "fiduciary relationship" is very broad. It is founded upon the trust and confidence one party places in the other that each will act in good faith and with fairness toward each other. As a result of this special relationship of trust, confidence, and reliance, the law imposes a fiduciary duty on the parties to the agency relationship. Neither party in a fiduciary relationship is permitted to engage in acts that could prejudice or take unfair advantage of the other party.

An example of a fiduciary relationship is the relationship between an investment advisor and client.

The fiduciary relationship between principal and agent encompasses a number of other subduties owed by the agent to the principal. These include the duties of

|   |   |
|---|---|
| • good faith | • obedience |
| • reasonable care | • accountability |
| • loyalty | • notice. |

The duties of good faith, reasonable care, and loyalty mean that the agent will not take unfair advantage of the principal or engage in acts that might be detrimental to the principal. In other words, the agent must be fair and responsible in the acts performed for the principal and will not engage in self-dealing or attempt to obtain secret profits.

The duty of obedience requires the agent to comply with all lawful and reasonable instructions from the principal.

The agent must also account to the principal for any funds received by the agent on the principal's behalf. The principal's funds must be kept separate from those of the agent and not be **commingled**. If the agent fails to segregate the funds, the law will impose a **constructive trust**. A

**trust** – meaning a property interest held by one person for the benefit of another – is usually memorialized by a written instrument. But even without a trust instrument, the law will often create a trust for the principal's funds that the agent failed to segregate. The agent must hold those funds in trust for the principal until an accounting is provided to the principal or the funds are segregated.

The agent must notify the principal of all matters that come to the agent's knowledge that affect the subject of the agency. A presumption exists that the agent has fulfilled this duty of providing the principal with oral or written notification of material information.

As a general rule, knowledge within the scope of the agency possessed by the agent is imputed to the principal. It is presumed that the principal knows what the agent does. The principal can be held liable to third parties for knowledge that the agent possesses but has not conveyed to the principal. The agent will be liable to the principal, in most cases, for whatever damage or loss the principal might suffer as a result of the agent's breach of this duty.

Damages may be **legal**, involving monetary repayment, or **equitable**. Examples of legal damages are actual damages – the true amount of loss – or punitive damages, which are invoked to punish the wrongdoer. Equitable damages come into play when only action, not money, will remedy the situation, such as returning an item of sentimental value to the owner.

*Principal's Duties*

The principal, in turn, owes duties to the agent:

- compensation
- a reasonably safe workplace
- reasonably safe equipment.

Unless the parties agree otherwise, the principal must compensate the agent for work performed and then reimburse the agent for expenses or losses reasonably incurred in furtherance of the agency relationship. The principal must also provide a reasonably safe workplace and reasonably safe equipment.

The principal's responsibility for failure to comply with these duties may be limited if the agent is negligent or assumes the risk of injury. Workers' compensation, a form of insurance for the principal, may mitigate the monetary liability of the principal for failing to provide reasonably safe working conditions and equipment.

## Important Terms

| | |
|---|---|
| Agency | Fiduciary relationship |
| Agent | Legal capacity |
| Constructive trust | Principal |
| Duties of agent | Statute of Frauds |
| Duties of principal | |

## Important Concepts

The agent acts on behalf of the principal and is subject to the control of the principal.

The principal controls the agent and is liable for certain acts of the agent.

The agent and principal have a fiduciary relationship in which neither must engage in acts that prejudice or take unfair advantage of the other.

---

# Chapter Two

# MORE BASIC CONCEPTS
# OF AGENCY

---

## Types of Agency Relationships

There are two basic types of agents: **general** and **special**.

A **general agent** is given a number of tasks to perform for the principal over an indefinite period of time. A general agent continues to perform the same types of acts over and over again in conjunction with new tasks that have been assigned to the general agent by the principal. Most employees act as general agents.

A **special agent**, on the other hand, has a finite set of tasks to perform. Upon completion of these tasks, the special agent's function ceases, and the agency relationship ends. A person hired to work on a specific project (a/k/a, a "temp") is an example of a special agent.

The amount of discretion the agent has does not determine whether the agent is special or general. Instead, the following factors are examined:

- the number of tasks to be performed
- the number of people with whom the agent must deal
- the length of time required for completion and
- whether or not the agency ceases upon completion of the tasks.

## Types of Agency Authority

As a general rule, the principal will only be liable for the acts of the agent if the agent acted with **authority**.

Whether or not one acts as an agent in performing a particular act turns upon

- the nature of the act performed and

- the existence of the authority possessed by the actor.

An agent can possess several types of authority, but the first issue is whether the agent has authority of *any* type. The types of authority the agent may have are:

- Actual Authority
    - Express
    - Implied
- Apparent Authority
- Inherent Authority.

*Actual Authority*

We have grouped express and implied authority as subcategories of actual authority because both are based on consent, either explicit or implicit, given by the principal to the agent's conduct.

**Express authority** is authority given by the principal to the agent that is specifically stated by the principal, either orally or in writing.

**Implied authority** is authority that the agent reasonably believes he or she has as a result of actions of the principal. It is based on circumstantial evidence and includes those powers necessary and proper to conduct the business of the principal. Implied authority "fills in the gaps" where the principal fails to specify every last detail of what the agent's powers should be to accomplish the tasks to be performed.

Implied authority may arise in the following ways:

- incidental
- custom and usage
- emergency or
- acquiescence.

**Incidental authority** is the authority to use all means reasonably necessary to fulfill the express agency agreement. For example, the manager of a department store has incidental authority to hire sales clerks and order supplies.

Authority to act may arise in accordance with generally accepted **custom or usage**. If a person wearing a nametag is standing behind a counter and asks "May I help you?," one may reasonably assume that person is an employee of the store.

An agent who has no specific directions as to what should be done in an emergency may take reasonably necessary measures of **emergency authority** when immediate action is required by the agent in order to protect the interests of the principal. If a fire breaks out in the store, an employee may act with emergency authority, smash a window open, and order the customers out.

When the principal acquiesces to, or does not object to, the repeated unauthorized acts of the agent, the agent could reasonably believe he or she has authority to perform the same acts in the future. ("But I've done this for months, and you never complained.")

The ambiguity of what is "customary," "necessary," "proper," or "reasonable" under the circumstances often leads to litigation concerning the scope of implied authority.

*Apparent Authority*

The second major category of authority is **apparent** or **ostensible authority**. Unlike actual authority, apparent authority is not based upon consent but is rather based upon the *appearance* of authority to the third party.

Apparent authority occurs when the principal, by word or conduct, represents to a third party that the agent has more authority than the agent actually has and, consequently, the third party reasonably relies on the principal's representations.

The appearance of authority can also arise when the principal fails to speak or act to contravene the appearance of authority created by the agent or another person. Even if the principal never intended for the agent to be authorized to take some action, the principal can still be bound by the agent's conduct if the principal

- knowingly permitted the agent to hold himself, herself, or itself out as having such authority, or

- failed to prevent the third party from believing that the agent had authority to act.

In these situations, the principal is not permitted to deny the existence of the authority, because such a denial would be unjust and detrimental to the relying third party. For example, in the presence of the store owner, the store manager – who has no actual authority to contract for improvements to the store – tells a building contractor that he or she has the authority to contract for an addition to the store. If the store owner says nothing to refute this, the store manager now has apparent authority to contract with the building contractor for improvements to the store.

*Inherent Authority*

The final category of authority, **inherent authority**, binds the principal for the agent's acts even though the agent has no actual or apparent authority. The rule applies when the principal puts the agent in a position to deal with unsuspecting third parties.

For example, an agent might see a business opportunity for which it has no authority to negotiate. The agent chooses to seize the opportunity for the principal without consulting the principal or disclosing the agency to the third party. Rather than place hardship on the innocent third party, the principal will be held liable for the acts of the agent.

**Liability of Principals and Agents**

The central question in the application of agency law is determining whether the principal should be liable for the acts of the agent. The answer turns on the agreement of the parties and the effect on third parties.

A principal's liability for its agent's acts is the price the principal pays for the control that the principal exercises over the actions of the agent. Quite simply, it is a trade-off.

The two major theories of liability for breach of an agency duty arise under **contract** and **tort**.

*Contract Theory*

A **contract** is a legally enforceable agreement between two or more parties. (See the authors' *Introduction to Contracts*.)

A contract is breached if a party violates its terms and conditions. The most common remedy for breach is to sue for monetary damages resulting from the breach.

What is the potential liability for each party to a contract made by an agent on behalf of the principal?

With respect to the principal's liability:

•     If the agent had authority to enter into the contract on behalf of the principal, the principal is bound by the contract and is liable to the third party for its breach.

•     If the agent lacked authority, the principal is not bound by the contract unless the principal subsequently ratifies the acts of the agent.

With respect to the agent's liability:

•     If the agent had authority and disclosed the existence of the agency and the identity of the principal to the third party, the agent is not bound by the contract with the third party and is not liable for the breach of that contract.

•     If the agent had authority but did not disclose both (a) the existence of the agency and (b) the identity of the principal, the agent, as well as the principal, is bound by the contract with the third party. Both are liable for the breach of that contract.

• If the agent has no authority, the agent may be bound by the contract with the third party, but the principal is not bound.

To avoid this result, an agent entering into contracts on behalf of a principal should make it perfectly clear, preferably in writing, that the agent is contracting for a principal. Sometimes the contract itself reflects an agent's status as the representative of a principal by language under the signature line.

With respect to the liability of the third party, the third party is generally bound by the contract and liable to the principal for breach of that contract.

For example: an agent, acting for a principal, enters into a contract with a third party. The agent tells the third party that he or she is acting as an agent and not in the agent's own behalf. The agent signs any documents with his or her name followed by the title "Agent for [Principal's Name]."

If the principal refuses to pay for the contracted product, the principal is liable to the third party for breaching the contract. The agent, however, is not liable for the principal's breach, because the agent has made full disclosure to the third party.

If the third party in the same situation breaches the contract, the third party is liable to the principal but not the agent.

To change the scenario, suppose the agent tells the third party that the agent is acting for a principal whose identity the agent cannot disclose. As before, the agent signs any documents with the title "Agent."

Because the identity of the principal is not disclosed, the third party must rely entirely on the agent. Both the principal and the agent are bound by the contract. The third party, however, is liable only to the principal.

*Tort Theory*

One of the most important concepts in the law is that a principal should, in some cases, be liable to a third party who is damaged as a result of torts committed by the principal's agent.

A *tort* is a civil wrong other than a breach of contract. It has four elements:

1. a legal duty,
2. a violation of the legal duty,
3. proximate cause, and
4. damages resulting from the violation of the duty.

**Proximate cause** means that the damages suffered resulted from the violation of the legal duty. Examples of common occurrences that include allegations of tortious conduct are automobile accidents, malpractice, and products liability.

The general rule in torts is that each person is liable for his or her own torts. Agency law contains an exception to this rule called *respondeat superior* or " let the master answer." The term derives from feudal times and refers to the responsibility of the master for the torts of a servant.

The rule does not imply, however, that the principal did anything wrong. It is simply an extension of the trade-off between control and liability that occurs in the agency relationship.

Whether the principal will be liable for the torts of the agent depends upon whether the agent committed the tort within the **course and scope of employment** for the principal. If so, the principal will be liable for the tort.

Generally, the tort is within the course and scope of employment if

- it occurred while the agent was working for the principal (course of employment); and

- it is something the agent might reasonably do during work (scope of employment).

The particular facts surrounding the conduct control whether the act is within the course and scope of employment. If an employee making assigned deliveries for his or her employer has an auto accident, the employer may be liable for any damages if the employee's negligence caused the accident. If, however, the accident occurred while the employee was on the way to a destination unrelated to his or her work (commonly called an "unauthorized frolic"), such as a friend's party, the employee would have sole liability. An employer would not be liable for such damages because the act occurred outside the scope of employment.

**The Independent Contractor**

The principal is liable only for the torts of a **"servant"** who is subject to the principal's control. An example of an agent that is not necessarily a servant is an **independent contractor**, a person who is hired by an employer to complete a specific task or project.

An example of this situation would be a freelance writer engaged for a specified fee to write a single article for a magazine. The parallel servant would be the magazine's staff writer who receives a variety of assignments and is compensated with salary and benefits.

In today's business climate, independent contractors offer a multitude of services. An attorney, paralegal, or accountant may be engaged to work on a specific, short-term project that requires a high degree of skill and knowledge. It is common for a retired executive to offer consultant services in his or her field of expertise as an independent contractor.

An independent contractor is generally less subject to the control of the employer than is a regular employee. An independent contractor often does not work on the employer's premises or utilize the employer's equipment.

Sometimes the distinction between an independent contractor and a servant is blurred. In deciding whether an independent contractor is actually a servant, a court will consider the following factors:

- Is the independent contractor subject to the control of the hiring party?

- Does the hiring party's control include the manner and method of performance of the independent contractor's task or tasks?

If the answers are yes, then the independent contractor is a servant, and the principal will be liable for his, her, or its torts.

It is important – both to the one who retains an independent contractor's services and the independent contractor – to establish that no employer/employee relationship exists. Besides the liability question, taxation can be an issue. The true independent contractor will be paid a set fee for his or her services, with no withholding for taxes, Social Security, or benefits. It is the responsibility of the independent contractor to see that appropriate taxes are tendered and to provide for items such as retirement plans.

At the same time, the independent contractor may need some degree of authority from the principal in order to carry out the tasks in an appropriate manner. If supplies must be ordered, for example, the third party supplier must rely on the independent contractor ordering the necessary supplies as an authorized agent of the principal.

Alternatively, of course, the independent contractor may furnish its own supplies and materials, but this solution is not always the most cost-effective, nor does it provide the most consistent quality control. At a building site, for example, it may be more thrifty to purchase materials in bulk than have each subcontractor supply his or her own.

**General Liability for Torts**

An employer/principal is generally not liable for damages caused by the intentional torts, such as assault or battery, of an employee/agent

because intentional torts are not within the scope of employment. But if
the master directs or allows the servant to commit an intentional tort, the
master will be held liable.

Liability, whether in tort or in contract, is an issue to be considered by
the independent contractor who retains its own subagents. For example,
a sole proprietor/independent contractor with no employees finds
himself or herself overwhelmed with work. Unable to find hours in a day
to complete all the tasks, but loath to give up the clients or disappoint
them, the sole proprietor/independent contractor retains its own
subagents. Under agency theory, the sole proprietor/independent
contractor then becomes a principal with all the accompanying liabilities
for acts of the principal's agent.

## Ratification

To determine whether the principal is bound by the acts of the agent, one
should examine not only the authority of the agent but also the acts of
the principal that could be construed as ratification. **Ratification**, the
confirmation of a **voidable** act (meaning a promise one may lawfully
decline to honor), is important in determining whether or not the
principal is liable for the agent's acts, whether contract or tort.

Ordinarily, if the agent did not have authority to act for the principal,
there is no liability on behalf of the principal. If, however, the principal
accepts, confirms, and ratifies the act, the principal has, in retrospect,
given the agent authority to act as he or she did. By so doing, the
principal will be bound by the act.

## Termination of the Agency Relationship

The termination of an agency relationship, like its creation, is relatively
simple. It can end by

- agreement of the parties or
- fulfillment of the purpose of the agency.

Either party can unilaterally terminate the agency relationship but may face a breach of contract suit. The agency can also be terminated automatically by operation of law, such as by the death or loss of capacity of either party.

## Important Terms

| | |
|---|---|
| Acquiescence | Implied authority |
| Actual authority | Incidental authority |
| Apparent authority | Independent contractor |
| Contract | Inherent authority |
| Custom and usage authority | Ratification |
| Emergency authority | *Respondeat superior* |
| Express authority | Special agent |
| General agent | Tort |

## Important Concepts

The principal is bound by the contractual acts of the agent if the agent had authority or if the principal ratifies the act or acts.

The agent is liable, along with the principal, if the agent had authority to enter into a contract but failed to disclose the agency.

The principal is liable for the torts of the agent committed within the course and scope of employment.

# Chapter Three

# TYPES OF BUSINESS ORGANIZATIONS

A business entity is an organization that has a separate legal existence. Different types of entities are available to the person who wants to operate a business. Each may create an agency relationship with the entity as the principal.

## Which to Choose?

The operator of a business, preferably upon the advice of legal counsel and an accountant, should select the entity that best suits his or her requirements. The owner should consider these factors:

- number of participants in the entity
- type of business to be carried out (products? services? both?)
- source and amount of funds available for creation and operation
- amount of liability the owners are willing to risk
- type of management desired
- tax consequences and
- transferability of interests in the business.

## What Are the Choices?

The best-known types of business organizations are the **sole proprietorship**, the **partnership**, and the **corporation**.

Partnerships may be **general** or **limited**. There is also a status called the **registered limited liability partnership**.

Variations on the business corporation include the **close corporation**, the **professional corporation**, and the **nonprofit corporation**.

The **limited liability company** and the **professional limited liability company** have become popular entities in recent years.

Another type of entity is the **association**, which is composed of members who join together to perform specific services or activities. A **cooperative association** is an association formed by a nonprofit purpose, such as a homeowners' association at a condominium. Another example is a grocery-purchasing association through which various vendors sell goods to members of the association, who in turn pay for a membership.

**The First Steps**

Formation of the business organization may require an agreement between the parties, various organizational formalities, payment of fees, use of certain titles in the entity's name, and periodic reports. Where a statutory scheme regulates the particular form of business entity, the controlling agreement governs only to the extent it does not conflict with statutory provisions.

**Limiting Liability**

A major concern in selecting the form of a business is the **personal liability** the owner or operator could incur – that is, liability that goes beyond the investment in the business and reaches one's personal assets. Personal liability is a major factor in choosing a form of doing business. Taxation and centralized management are also important factors.

**How Long Will the Entity Last?**

A sole proprietorship exists at the pleasure of its sole proprietor. It is the easiest form of business to begin and end.

Partnerships, whether general or limited, and limited liability companies do not have continuity of existence. This is an important concept in the taxation of these entities, none of which are taxed at the entity level. Instead, they enjoy " **flow-through**" or " **pass-through**" taxation, by which profits and losses flow through the entity to the partners or to the members, as the case may be, and are taxed at the individual's own tax rate.

Corporations are deemed, both by state statutes and by the federal Internal Revenue Service (IRS) regulations, to have continuity of existence. A corporation will continue to exist until it is dissolved either voluntarily, by the authority of its shareholders or directors, or involuntarily, by an outside authority such as a bankruptcy court or a secretary of state.

Generally, a business will terminate when its management is no longer available to continue the business. Unless otherwise provided by the controlling agreement, the business can also be dissolved at any time by the agreement of the owners.

## Important Terms

| | |
|---|---|
| Association | Pass-through taxation |
| Business corporation | Personal liability |
| Close corporation | Professional corporation |
| Entity | Professional limited liability |
| Flow-through taxation | company |
| General partnership | Registered limited liability |
| Limited partnership | partnership |
| Limited liability company | Sole proprietorship |

## Important Concepts

The choice of operational form should be based upon these factors:

- insulation from personal liability
- tax consequences
- type of management desired
- transferability of interest
- number of participants
- type of business
- start-up and sustaining capital.

The main categories of business organizations are

- sole proprietorships
- associations
- partnerships
- corporations and
- limited liability companies.

# Chapter Four

# THE SOLE PROPRIETORSHIP

Every day around the nation, persons open businesses in the form of the sole proprietorship. It remains the most simple and popular form of business organization. One reason it remains so simple is that frequently the sole proprietorship is not governed by any specific statute, plus there is the lure of self-employment and being one's own boss.

An advantage of the sole proprietorship form of doing business is that its profits are taxed once, at the individual level. Profits of the business are taxed as income to the owner, while losses or expenses of the business are deductible by the owner.

The sole proprietorship requires only one person – the sole proprietor – who may or may not choose to hire employees. In terms of agency law, the sole proprietor and the employees are agents of the sole proprietorship.

Management of a sole proprietorship is centralized in the sole proprietor. Because the personal assets of the sole proprietor are used to run the business, those assets are therefore subject to the claims of creditors. No insulation from personal liability exists. All of the business debts are personal debts of the sole proprietor. Only insurance, such as theft or liability, can protect the sole proprietor and his or her assets.

**Appropriate Documents**

A sole proprietorship may need to obtain, prepare, or file one or more of the following documents:

- Form SS-4
- Assumed name certificate (also known as a fictitious business name filing, or "doing business as," or d/b/a)

- Sales tax permit
- License

*Form SS-4*

Even though profits and losses of the sole proprietorship are reported on the tax return of the sole proprietor, sole proprietors are frequently required to obtain a separate federal employer identification number (FEIN) for the sole proprietorship before a lending institution will lend funds to the sole proprietorship.

The number is obtained by filing the federal Form SS-4, a copy of which may be obtained at any Internal Revenue Service office or downloaded from the home page of the IRS at www.ustreas.irs.gov. The IRS will also furnish an instruction sheet explaining how the FEIN number may be obtained by phone by calling a regional IRS office.

Even if you obtain the FEIN by phone, the original signed form must be sent to the IRS promptly by regular mail or fax. There is no filing fee.

*Assumed Name Certificate*

Frequently a sole proprietor will conduct his or her business under an assumed name, also called a fictitious business name. The sole proprietor may (or must – check with your state) file an assumed name certificate that sets forth the name under which he or she will be doing business, particularly if the name implies that more than one person is involved (as, "Jones & Associates").

The assumed name certificate is usually filed in the office of the recorder or the clerk in the county or counties in which the sole proprietorship is doing business. Such a certificate usually will include:

- the assumed name under which the business is or is to be conducted or rendered
- the period during which the assumed name will be used
- the name and address of the sole proprietor

- the principal office address of the sole proprietorship
- the county or counties where the business is being, or is to be, conducted under such assumed name.

The certificate may or may not require notarization, depending upon the statutes. The fee is determined by the agency where the certificate is filed.

Most agencies provide for filing an amendment to or an abandonment of the assumed name should circumstances make such a filing appropriate. A renewal may be required if the end of the filing period is approaching.

*Sales Tax Permit*

If the sole proprietorship offers products or services on which the state collects point-of-sale taxes, it must apply for a sales tax permit and collect and remit such sales taxes to the appropriate authorities.

*License*

If the sole proprietor is engaging in an endeavor that requires licensure, the sole proprietorship must apply for the appropriate license. For example, a liquor license would be required if the sole proprietorship intends to sell alcoholic beverages. A cosmetologist, the operator of a day care center, a physician – all require licensure before services can be offered to the public.

**Changing to an Incorporated Entity**

If the sole proprietor wants to terminate the sole proprietorship but to continue the same business under the same name in another manner – particularly as a corporation – some states require a public filing in a **newspaper of general circulation**.

A newspaper of general circulation is one that is readily available to the public in the community where the publishing entity does business.

"Readily available" is interpreted to mean for sale on a newsstand or by delivery to homes in the community.

The notice may read something like this:

Notice of Intent to Incorporate

Notice is hereby given that [name of sole proprietorship], a sole proprietorship, whose principal office is at [address], [name of county] County, [intends to incorporate/has incorporated] without a change of business name.

[Name of Sole Proprietorship]

## Section 351 of the Internal Revenue Code

Such a notice of intent to incorporate is often called a "**351 filing**" after the section of the Internal Revenue Code that permits, under certain circumstances, a transition from an unincorporated to an incorporated form of doing business to be a tax-free event.

## Termination of a Sole Proprietorship

A sole proprietorship will terminate at the death or incapacity of the sole proprietor. He or she can also decide to stop operating the business at any time, thereby terminating the sole proprietorship. Aside from personal liability, termination by death or incapacity is the greatest risk associated with this form of business.

## Important Terms

Assumed name certificate
d/b/a
FEIN
Fictitious business name
Form SS-4

Newspaper of general circulation
Personal liability
Section 351

## Important Concepts

The sole proprietorship is the simplest organizational form but affords no insulation from personal liability.

The sole proprietorship terminates upon the sole proprietor's death, disability, or decision to discontinue business.

---

# Chapter Five

# THE GENERAL PARTNERSHIP

---

A primary purpose in creating a partnership is to make and distribute profits through a business form that is taxed only once.

## Creation

A general partnership has five elements:

1.   the voluntary association
2.   of two or more persons (called general partners or partners)
3.   to carry on business
4.   for profit
5.   as co-owners.

Who are the two or more "persons" that can be members of a general or limited partnership? Most partnership statutes define "persons" to include not only individuals but also entities. Thus, a corporation, individual, trustee, or even another partnership may be a general or limited partner. To be a partner, an individual must have legal capacity.

These persons form a partnership to carry on business. A partnership is generally an ongoing business; it will not cease to exist at the completion of a specified task.

This continuity of existence contrasts with a similar form of business known as a **joint venture**. A joint venture is purposefully created to complete a specific task or tasks and will terminate thereafter. It resembles the special agent in agency theory in that, once the required task is performed, the relationship between the parties ends.

The formation of a general partnership requires an agreement between the members. The agreement may be oral, written, or implied. The elements of the agreement must be those found in the statutory definition of the general partnership. The partnership agreement can contain other terms agreed upon by the partners so long as these do not conflict with statutory requirements.

Although most partnership acts do not provide for any statutory filing, courts will not find that a partnership has been formed unless the parties intended to create a entity that meets requirements of their state's definition of a general partnership.

Often persons believe they have formed a general partnership simply because they have shared the profits of a business. Indeed, many partnership statutes state that the sharing of profits is *prima facie* evidence that the recipient is a partner in the business. The acts may also state, however, that payments for a debt, wages, annuity, interest on a loan, or sale of goodwill do not constitute profits and do not fall into the category of *prima facie* evidence of a partnership's existence.

*The Written Partnership Agreement*

Although a written partnership agreement is not always required by statute for the formation of a general partnership, it is a wise idea to reduce the terms of the partnership to writing. Certain provisions should always be included.

The agreement should specifically identify the statute under which the partnership is formed. The name of the partnership, of course, should also be stated in the agreement.

An often neglected portion of the partnership agreement is the purpose section. Drafters of partnership agreements often fail to remember the doctrine of agency law that a principal is bound by the acts of the agent if the agent has authority. If the agreement contains a very broad purpose clause, there is a greater likelihood that the partnership (the principal) will be bound by the acts of the partner (the agent) than if a narrow purpose is stated, because those acts will more likely fall within the course and scope of the partnership and the partner will have authority. Authority raises, in turn, the aspect of liability described in the previous chapters on agency.

A specific purpose clause will limit the authority available to the partners and narrow the exposure of the partnership and its members to liability. The agreement may be amended in the event the purpose of the partnership changes or expands.

Another frequently neglected provision of the partnership agreement is the duration clause. If no specific term is stated in the agreement, a partnership-at-will is created, and the partners may dissolve the partnership at any time without violating the agreement. It is, therefore, wise to state that the partnership will continue until a date certain unless terminated sooner by the terms of the agreement.

In order to prevent the unwanted involvement of third parties in the partnership, the partnership agreement should also limit the ability of a partner to transfer his, her, or its partnership interest.

Partnership agreement provisions require the most careful drafting when covering

- the distribution of profits and losses
- the events and conditions for withdrawal and
- the dissolution, continuation, and winding up.

The content will depend upon the needs and sophistication of the partners and the partnership.

*Assumed Name of a General Partnership*

Unless all of the names of the general partners are contained in the name of the general partnership, an assumed name certificate generally must be filed with the appropriate state or county authority. The certificate usually includes the following information:

- assumed name of the partnership
- name and office address of the partnership

- name and address of each general partner
- duration of the use of the assumed name.

The assumed name certificate is the same certificate that must be filed by a sole proprietorship that transacts business under an assumed name. In both instances, the certificate serves to put third parties on notice of the identity of the parties behind the business.

An assumed name certificate must be renewed periodically and within a specific time after any event that causes the information in the certificate to become materially misleading. A partnership that fails to comply with these requirements may not be able to sue or defend a lawsuit as a partnership and may be subject to criminal penalties for a willful failure to comply with the assumed name statute.

## Operation

*Authority*

A general partnership is formed by two or more persons. Under agency theory and as set forth in the partnership statutes, every partner is an agent for the partnership, and every partner's act that is within the scope of the partnership business will bind the partnership unless

- the partner has no authority, or
- the third party knew that the partner did not have authority.

Agency theories are also applicable in determining contractual and tort liability of the partnership form of doing business. Each partner is jointly and severally liable for the debts and obligations of the partnership. **Joint and several liability** means that the partners are collectively and individually liable for the debts and obligations of the partnership.

Moreover, a partner's wrongful act or omission committed during the ordinary course of the business will cause the partnership to be liable.

## Fiduciary Duties

Each general partner owes fiduciary duties to the other partners and to the partnership. Joint and several liability is imposed on each partner who breaches these duties.

Fiduciary duties are broadly construed for partners. For example, most partnership statutes require each partner to account to the partnership for "any benefit." Each partner must also hold in trust any profits arising from partnership transactions or from the uses of partnership property.

Moreover, a partner must offer to the partnership any opportunities that the partner knows fall within the purpose of the partnership. This is called the **partnership opportunity doctrine**. (This doctrine is very similar to the business opportunity rule discussed in Chapter Thirteen in connection with corporations.) Its function is to prevent conflicts of interest and maintain compliance with the intent of fiduciary duties: fair dealing and honesty.

Duty has its limits, however, and a partner is not totally precluded from conducting individual transactions. The partner may, for example, profit from individual investments or from unrelated types of activities, such as teaching, even in an area in which the partnership operates.

## Property Rights

Partners are co-owners of the business and share profits. The property rights of a partner are

- rights in specific partnership property
- interests in the partnership and
- rights to participate in the management.

The partners hold partnership property as **tenants in common**. Upon the death of a partner, that partner's rights in specific partnership property go to the remaining partners. The partner's right in specific partnership property cannot be attached or used to satisfy claims other than claims against the partnership, because a partner has the right to possess partnership property for partnership purposes only.

Unless provided otherwise in the partnership agreement, a partner may transfer or assign his, her, or its interest in the partnership. The transferee does not, however, become a partner but merely receives the transferring partner's share of the profits.

In addition, unless provided otherwise in an agreement, partners

- have an equal voice in management of the partnership;
- approve ordinary partnership matters by majority vote;
- share profits or losses equally;
- do not receive compensation for services rendered to the partnership; and
- may withdraw from the partnership at any time.

It is not uncommon in larger partnerships for some management tasks and some types of decisions to be delegated to a smaller group or subcommittee of partners.

*Indemnification*

Each partner is indemnified by the partnership for payments made and personal liabilities incurred to conduct partnership business or to preserve the partnership. The partner is entitled to reimbursement from the partnership for such expenses. For example, travel and entertainment expenses incurred by a partner in promoting the business are reimbursable if they were reasonable and appropriate for the business involved.

**Termination**

*Dissolution*

The **dissolution** of a partnership is the change in the relation of the partners caused by any partner ceasing to be associated with the partnership. Note that this is simply a change in legal relationships and is not synonymous with **termination**. If there is a dissolution (for example, on the death of a partner), the partnership continues until the **winding up** (**liquidation** and payment of creditors). This "winding up" terminates the partnership. The partnership agreement, however, may provide that certain events, such as a partner's death, will not trigger dissolution but will allow the partnership to continue.

A general partnership usually continues at will until dissolved by the partners. A general partnership will, however, dissolve by operation of law on the occurrence of any of the following events:

- death of a partner
- insolvency of a partner
- expulsion of a partner
- court-ordered termination or
- the business of the partnership becoming unlawful.

In addition to the dissolution of a general partnership by operation of law, a general partner may petition the court to dissolve the general partnership. The court may dissolve the partnership under any of the following conditions:

- if a partner
  - becomes incompetent or insane, or
  - engages in misconduct, or
  - breaches the partnership agreement; or

- if the partnership can only be carried on at a loss; or

- for any equitable reason.

Partner misconduct upon which the court can dissolve the general partnership is conduct that prejudicially affects the operation of the business. Likewise, the acts of breach must be willful or persistent conduct that makes it reasonably impossible to operate the business.

The general partnership agreement can provide other conditions for dissolution of the partnership. As with a limited partnership, on

dissolution of a general partnership, the remaining partners may
continue or wind up the business, subject to any terms of the
partnership agreement.

*Winding Up*

Winding up is the official termination of the business by a two-step
process: (1) liquidation of partnership assets and (2) payment of
creditors.

Unless the partnership agreement provides otherwise, those partners
who have not wrongfully dissolved the general partnership have the
right to wind up the partnership affairs.

Upon termination, the liabilities of a general partnership are paid in an
order specified in the partnership act. For example:

- debts owed to creditors other than partners
- debts owed to partners who are creditors
- capital contributions returned to partners and
- debts owed to partners as profits.

Usually all of the liabilities in each category must be paid before the
next category of creditor is reached for payment. The **capital
contribution** of a partner is that partner's investment in the
partnership. Partners can have different degrees of ownership and the
capital can take different forms, such as cash, equipment, real estate,
and specialized skill or effort.

## Important Terms

Assumed name

Capital contribution

Dissolution

Partnership agreement

Partnership-at-will

Partnership opportunity doctrine

Person

Tenant in common

To carry on business

Winding up

## Important Concepts

A partnership is a voluntary association of two or more persons to carry on business for profit as co-owners.

Partnerships are created by an oral or written agreement that embodies purposes and terms of the partnership.

General partners are jointly and severally liable for the debts and obligations of the partnership.

Unlike the dissolution of a corporation, which means termination of the entity, the dissolution of a partnership is a change in the relation of the partners caused by any partner's ceasing to be associated with the partnership.

Upon an event triggering dissolution, the partnership may either continue or wind up.

---

# Chapter Six

# THE LIMITED PARTNERSHIP

---

A limited partnership is basically a general partnership, but it must have at least one general partner and one limited partner. In most states, it must file a **certificate of limited partnership** with the appropriate state agency, usually the secretary of state.

Like general partnerships, limited partnerships are governed by the common law principles of agency and by statutory law.

The primary motivations of an investor in a limited partnership are single taxation and limited liability. The investor's profits from his, her or its investment are taxed only once. The investor, as a limited partner, is also insulated from personal liability for expenses and obligations of the business. A limited partner can lose only the amount the limited partner invested in the limited partnership.

## Creation

*Certificate of Limited Partnership*

To form a limited partnership, one or more general partners and one or more limited partners must enter into an agreement. As in a general partnership, the limited partnership agreement may be oral or written. If the agreement is in writing, it should contain, at a minimum, the information required to be filed with the state agency.

All general partners must execute a certificate of limited partnership, which is then filed with the state. A certificate of limited partnership must generally provide:

- the name of the limited partnership
- the name and address of each general partner
- the name of the registered agent and the address of the registered office, and

- the address of the principal place of business.

The purpose of the certificate is to provide public notice of basic information concerning the limited partnership.

*The Written Partnership Agreement*

If a written partnership agreement is not required by statute for the formation of the limited partnership, the partners' agreement may still be – and usually is – reduced to writing. For basic provisions, see the preceding chapter on general partnerships.

When a limited partnership is formed, the name must include a form of the words "limited" and "partnership" or the abbreviation "L.P." or "Ltd." at the end of its name.

The limited partnership name may not contain the name of a limited partner unless

- that name is also the name of a general partner, or
- the business of the limited partnership has been carried on under that name before the admission of that limited partner.

The limited partnership's name cannot imply that it engages in a business other than that stated in its purpose. Nor can the name be deceptively similar to the name of another limited partnership, corporation, or limited liability company already formed or qualified in the state.

The fiduciary standards applicable to the general partners in a general partnership are also applicable to the general partner(s) in a limited partnership.

Unlike a general partner, however, a limited partner cannot participate in the management of the partnership. The limited liability of a limited partner is predicated on his, her, or its nonparticipation in the management of the limited partnership. Nonetheless, the types of conduct in which a limited partner may engage without affecting such partner's limited liability are expanding. This conduct includes:

- acting as an employee, agent, or contractor for the limited partnership or as an officer, director or shareholder of a corporate general partner

- acting as a consultant for the limited partnership

- acting as a surety, guarantor, or endorser for the limited partnership

- calling or participating in a meeting of the partners

- serving on a committee of the limited partnership

- winding up the partnership

- dealing with derivative actions on behalf of the limited partnership

- voting, proposing, approving or disapproving matters having to do with the vital interests of the partnership, such as sales of assets, refinancing, admitting or removing general or limited partners.

A limited partner who does participate in management assumes the same personal liability that is imposed on a general partner. The limited partner thus must balance the need to promote and protect his, her, or its investment against the possibility of exposure to personal liability for participating in management decisions. A similar concept in connection with corporations – that of the corporate alter ego – is discussed in Chapter Twelve.

Just what, then, is the extent of a limited partner's liability? Unless the limited partner is also a general partner or participates in the control of the partnership, the limited partner's liability is restricted to the amount of his, her or its investment. In other words, the limited partner is not personally liable for the debts of the limited partnership. General partners are, however, personally liable.

## Operation

The creation and subsequent operation of a limited partnership creates a fiduciary relationship among the participants. General and limited partners owe fiduciary duties to each other and to the partnership. The partners must act in good faith and deal fairly with each other and the partnership.

Unless the partnership agreement provides otherwise, a limited partner may transfer his, her, or its interest in the limited partnership to another person or entity. The purchaser of the interest does not become a partner, however, and the selling partner remains a partner. The purchaser will, however, receive profits from the partnership and have the right to information concerning the partnership.

Each limited partner is taxed on a portion of the partnership profits and may deduct a portion of the partnership losses and expenses. The limited partnership itself is not taxed. A limited partnership must maintain certain records and make these records available after receipt of a written request from a proper person.

If a limited partnership is an **at-will partnership** – one for which no specific duration is provided – a general partner may withdraw from the partnership at any time. The withdrawing partner must, however, give notice to the other partners of its withdrawal.

## Termination

A limited partnership will continue to exist until one of the following occurs:

- all of the partners agree to terminate,
- the agreement requires termination,
- the duration of the partnership is completed,
- the court orders a dissolution, or

- a general partner withdraws due to insolvency, death, or incompetency.

Under most partnership statutes, however, the limited partnership may be revived and continued.

As with a general partner, a limited partner may, after providing due notice, withdraw from the limited partnership at any time. The limited partner must, however, give a lengthy notice to each general partner. Unlike a general partnership, the limited partnership will not dissolve if a limited partner withdraws, becomes insolvent, dies, or is expelled.

In the event a general partner withdraws from the limited partnership in violation of the agreement, the partnership may sue for damages from that partner. Such damages include the costs suffered by the partnership to replace the withdrawn partner.

When the limited partnership decides to wind up, usually a certificate of cancellation must be filed with the appropriate state agency. It must be signed by all general partners participating in the winding up. If there are no general partners, then the certificate of cancellation must be signed by all nonpartner liquidators or by a those limited partners that together hold a majority of the partnership units.

Upon termination, the liabilities of the limited partnership will usually be paid in order as follows:

- debts owed to creditors who are not partners
- income owed to limited partners
- capital contributions returned to limited partners
- debts owed to creditors who are partners
- profits owed to general partners
- capital contributions returned to general partners.

Every creditor in each category must be paid before the next category of creditors can be paid. It is clear from this order that the limited partner receives preferential treatment on termination. This is because the limited partner does not take part in the management of the limited partnership. The general partners, though, must bear the financial burden of their decisions and are paid last.

## Important Terms

At-will partnership                         Limited partnership
Certificate of limited                      Management
   partnership

## Important Concepts

A limited partnership must complete and file a certificate of limited
   partnership with the appropriate state official.

General partners are jointly and severally liable for the debts and
   obligations of the limited partnership. Limited partners,
   however, have limited liability but will be treated as general
   partners if they engage in the management of the limited
   partnership.

A limited partner's potential liability is limited to its investment in the
   limited partnership.

# Chapter Seven

# THE REGISTERED LIMITED LIABILITY PARTNERSHIP

One of the major disadvantages of doing business as a partnership is that an individual partner is not necessarily insulated from liability for the wrongful acts of another partner. To mitigate this problem, states have provided for registration as a limited liability partnership.

Legislatures have acknowledged that innocent partners should be insulated from liability for wrongful acts committed by other partners or employees.

Moreover, because the registered limited liability partnership may not be subject to franchise tax or foreign interpretation by other states, in some states it is a highly desirable status, utilized even if only two general partners are involved.

What is a **registered limited liability partnership**? Using the language found in the Texas Revised Partnership Act as an example,

> A partner in a registered limited liability partnership is not individually liable for debts and obligations of the partnership arising from errors, omissions, negligence, incompetence, or malfeasance committed … in the course of the partnership business by another partner or a representative of the partnership not working under the supervision or direction of the first partner. (TRPA § 3.08)

"**Representative**" includes an agent, servant, or employee of the registered limited liability partnership. Thus, partners are insulated from personal liability for wrongful acts committed by employees, as well as other partners. Moreover, a partner will be personally liable only for the covered wrongful acts if he or she was directly involved in the specific wrongful act or had notice or knowledge of the act(s) but failed to take reasonable steps to prevent or cure them.

The use of a registered limited liability partnership does not, however, affect any of the following:

- joint and several liability for a partner for debts and obligations of the partnership arising from any cause other than the covered wrongful acts,
- the liability of partnership to pay its debts and obligations out of partnership property, or
- the manner in which service of citation or other civil process may be served against a partnership.

**Creation**

Registered limited liability partnership is a status. First, a general (or limited – depending on what types of partnerships the state allows to register) partnership must be created. Then, it files an application for registration with the state. The application generally includes the following information:

- the name of the partnership
- its federal tax identification number
- the address of its principal office in state and out of state, if applicable
- the number of partners at the time of application
- a brief description of the partnership's business (as "the practice of law").

The registration will expire at the end of a specific period (often one year) after the date of registration or later effective date unless the registration is withdrawn, revoked, or renewed.

The registered limited liability partnership's name must contain the words "registered limited liability partnership" or the abbreviation "L.L.P." as the last words or letters of its name. The authorizing acts are usually silent as to whether notice of converting to a registered limited liability partnership is required. The best business practice would be, however, to notify existing creditors and clients.

The thinking behind the legislatures' move to provide for limitation of liability is that the public or the consumer will be protected by the required insurance. The registered limited liability partnership must carry a statutorily prescribed amount of liability insurance of a kind that is designed to cover the kinds of wrongful acts encompassed in the authorizing act. The registered limited liability partnership can also designate and segregate the amount of money in lieu of liability insurance by either:

- depositing cash, bank certificates of deposit, or U.S. Treasury obligations in a trust or bank escrow or
- obtaining a letter of credit.

The requirement of insurance is not admissible at trial and may not be made known to the jury in determining an issue of liability or damages.

**Operation**

The registered limited liability partnership operates in the same manner as any partnership that is not registered. Partners remain jointly and severally liable for the debts and obligations of the partnership arising from any other causes than those covered by the liability insurance.

In addition, partners are not vicariously liable for a partnership obligation arising under the following circumstances:

- if the culpable partner or representative whose conduct creates the liability is working under the supervision or direction of the partner when the misconduct occurs;

- if the partner is directly involved in the specific activity in which another partner or representative commits the misconduct; or

- if the partner has notice or knowledge of the misconduct at the time of the occurrence.

A person has **knowledge** of a fact when he or she is actually aware of the fact or when he or she has knowledge of such other facts as, in the circumstances, show bad faith.

A person has **notice** of a fact when the person claiming the benefit of the notice states the fact or delivers a written statement of the fact to the person being notified, or to a proper person at the place of business or residence of the person being notified. Constructive knowledge or imputed knowledge, which would normally apply under agency theory, does not apply in a registered limited liability partnership for purposes of determining notice or knowledge.

**Termination**

Generally, a registered limited liability partnership will terminate upon the consent of its partners or upon the expiration of its annual registration.

## Important Terms

Knowledge                                    RLLP
Notice                                       Vicarious liability
Representative

## Important Concepts

A registered limited liability partnership is a general or limited partnership that registers with the state to obtain the status of a registered limited liability partnership.

A registered limited liability partnership must obtain a statutorily prescribed liability insurance minimum for the covered acts.

Partners of a registered limited liability partnership are not liable for the debts and obligations of the partnership if they arise from:

- errors, omissions, negligence, incompetence, or malfeasance committed by a partner within the course of partnership business UNLESS

- the partner was directly involved in the act(s) or had notice or knowledge of them.

---

# Chapter Eight

# THE CORPORATION

---

A term that frequently comes to mind when people think of "business" is "corporation." A **corporation** is a legal entity created under statutory authority. The most common form is the general business corporation. Other types are the close corporation, the professional corporation, and the nonprofit corporation.

Some corporations are publicly owned – that is, their shares are traded on markets such as the New York Stock Exchange. Others are privately held by as few as one shareholder.

Most corporate businesses operate as general business corporations. Any lawful business for profit may organize under this form. Specialized businesses, such as banks or insurance companies, are organized and governed under other state or federal laws that apply specifically to those entities.

## The Close Corporation

A **close corporation**, sometimes called a **closely held corporation**, is a corporation that, having met the statutory requirements for creation, has elected a certain status that modifies the general business corporation form to allow for more flexible management and control. Its name derives from the fact that it is statutorily limited to a certain number of shareholders and its shares are not publicly traded. Corporations owned entirely by one family are often close corporations.

A close corporation relies on a **shareholders' agreement** to restrict shares getting into the hands of unwanted shareholders. The shareholders' agreement performs the same function as a partnership agreement in a partnership by defining the terms of operation and the roles and powers of the members. It must be executed by each shareholder and usually can only be amended by unanimous written approval of all of the shareholders.

The well-written shareholders' agreement will contemplate these events:

- the death of a shareholder who is a natural person
- the divorce of a shareholder who is a natural person
- the disability of a shareholder who is a natural person employed by the corporation
- the dissolution of a shareholder who is a statutory person
- the bankruptcy of a shareholder who is either a natural person or a statutory person and
- an offer to purchase shares tendered by an outsider to a shareholder.

The shareholders' agreement usually gives the corporation the **right of first refusal** to purchase a shareholder's shares when any of these events occur. The agreement will give the corporation 30 or 60 days to consider whether to purchase the shares. Should the corporation not exercise its right, the shareholders' agreement will give the right of next refusal to the other shareholders in proportion to shares they own.

It is customary to demand that the spouse of each shareholder execute a **spousal consent** to the shareholders' agreement to acknowledge that he or she has read the agreement and understands that he or she has no right to the shareholder's shares in the event of death or divorce.

In the event of a shareholder's death or disability, key-person insurance may be the source of funds for the corporation to purchase the shares. When a corporation repurchases its own shares that it has previously issued, they are known as **treasury shares**.

**The Professional Corporation**

A professional corporation is formed by persons who are licensed or otherwise authorized to render certain professional services. In your state, these professions may include:

accountants
acupuncturists
architects
athletic trainers
attorneys
audiologists
certified social workers
chiropractors
court reporters
dentists
educational diagnosticians
engineers
enrolled agents
insurance agents
interior designers
licensed counselors
licensed insurance adjusters
massage therapists
nurses
occupational therapists

optometrists
orthotists
paramedics
patent agents
pharmacists
physical therapists
physicians
podiatrists
private security investigators
prosthetists
psychologists
real estate agents or brokers
registered lobbyists
registered public surveyors
respiratory care therapists
securities broker/dealers
security investigators
social workers
speech pathologists
veterinarians

## The Nonprofit Corporation

The nonprofit, or not-for-profit, corporation is organized pursuant to state statutes but may apply for tax-exempt status under the Internal Revenue Code (IRC).

No income of a nonprofit corporation may be distributed to its members, directors, or officers. A nonprofit corporation can exist for cultural, charitable, educational, or other beneficial purposes as set forth in its enabling document.

In order to prevent an unscrupulous individual from holding himself or herself out as a church or charitable organization, statutes governing nonprofit corporations may have provisions for multiple leadership. For example, the statute may:

- require a board of directors with no fewer than three members, or

- forbid the same person from serving as both president and secretary of the corporation.

Depending on its purpose, the nonprofit corporation may wish to qualify under state law as a tax-exempt entity and obtain an identifying number that relieves it from paying merchant's state sales tax on its purchases. Details of applying for this status are available from the state's tax-collecting authority.

Incorporation under state law as a nonprofit corporation does not automatically bestow federal tax-exempt or tax-deductible status on the entity. If a nonprofit corporation wishes to qualify as a tax-deductible corporation under federal law, it must apply to the Internal Revenue Service (IRS).

Nonprofit corporations organized for charitable, benevolent, religious, or educational purposes will be colloquially called "**501(c)(3)**" entities, so named after the IRC section under which they qualify as entities to which donations are deductible to the donor. The term "**501(c)(6)**" denotes nonprofit corporations that qualify under IRC §501(c)(6) as trade associations.

When a nonprofit corporation pays its creditors and dissolves, its disposable assets may be directed only to an entity that has been approved as a 501(c)(3) corporation by the IRS. Under no circumstances may assets be distributed to members, directors, or agents of the dissolving entity.

If the nonprofit corporation has qualified with the IRS under any parts of the IRC, appropriate federal filings must be made when the nonprofit corporation dissolves.

**Advantages of the Corporate Form**

Factors that can motivate a business operator to select the corporate form include:

- insulation from personal liability
- centralized management
- continuity of existence and
- transferability of interest.

Because the corporation exists as a separate legal entity apart from its members, its owners – its shareholders or stockholders – enjoy **insulation from personal liability**. Officers, directors, and shareholders can only be held personally liable for their acts under very definite and narrow circumstances. If the business fails, the participants can walk away without having to pay business creditors from their personal assets.

The corporation offers **centralized management**. Policy decisions made by the board of directors are carried out by the officers.

A corporation has **continuity of existence**. Unlike a sole proprietorship or a partnership, a corporation does not terminate or dissolve upon the death or incapacity of its owners. A corporation continues to exist until it is voluntarily or involuntarily dissolved.

Unless such transfer is specifically restricted, shares of stock bear the **right of alienation** (the right to be sold or transferred) and are **freely transferrable**. The investor may purchase or sell at will. The exceptions in the close corporation have been mentioned above. Corporations that are not close corporations may, however, also initiate a shareholders' agreement that restricts ready transfer of the corporation's shares.

**Disadvantage of the Corporate Form**

If the corporate form is so great, why aren't we all using it to do business? The answer is double taxation.

The profits of a corporation are first taxed to the corporation and paid by the corporation. If the corporation passes its profits on to shareholders as dividends, each shareholder is taxed on the dividend received.

(There are, however, procedures to avoid this problem of double taxation, if the corporation qualifies. See Chapter Fourteen.)

## Creation

A corporation is an artificial person created by statute and organized for the purpose or purposes stated in its application for corporate existence.

A corporation comes into existence by filing a document – usually called **articles of incorporation**, but sometimes called a **certificate of incorporation** – with the secretary of state in its **state of domestication** – its "home" state.

## Operation

The policy of corporations is carried out by **officers**, who are elected by the **board of directors**. The board of directors, which sets policy, is in turn elected by the shareholders.

To be more precise, subsequent boards of directors are elected by the shareholders. The **initial board of directors** is named by the incorporator(s). That initial board then has authority to issue shares, an action that creates shareholders who, thereafter, elect subsequent boards of directors.

## Termination

A corporation continues to exist until it is formally dissolved, either voluntarily or involuntarily. It may outlive the natural persons who incorporated and managed it.

**Voluntary dissolution** is accomplished by filing **articles of dissolution** or a **certificate of dissolution**. This filing is not permitted until all appropriate taxes have been paid to the state.

**Involuntary dissolution** occurs upon the order of the court or the action of the secretary of state.

## Important Terms

Board of directors

Centralized management

Close corporation

Continuity of existence

Double taxation

Insulation from personal liability

Involuntary dissolution

Limited personal liability

Nonprofit corporation

Officers

Professional corporation

Right of first refusal

Section 501(c)(3)

Section 501(c)(6)

Shareholders

Shareholders' agreement

Treasury shares

Voluntary dissolution

## Important Concepts

A corporation is an artificial person created by statute and organized for the purpose or purposes stated in its articles of incorporation.

The advantages of the corporate form are

- insulation from personal liability
- centralized management
- continuity of existence and
- transferability of interest.

A corporation may be a

- general business corporation
- closely held corporation
- professional corporation or
- nonprofit corporation.

# Chapter Nine

# CREATION OF THE CORPORATION

A corporation comes into existence when a clerk at the filing agency assigns a unique number to the new entity and stamps the document of application "Filed" as of a certain date. The effective date of filing can be delayed if desired.

## Domestic, Foreign or Alien

Corporations can be categorized as domestic, foreign, or alien.

A **domestic corporation** is one doing business in the state in which it was incorporated. Although it may do business in many states, a corporation may incorporate under the laws of only one state.

A **foreign corporation** is one doing business in a state other than its state of incorporation. A corporation must **qualify to do business** by obtaining a **certificate of authority** under the laws of the host state. For example, if an Idaho corporation wants to do business in Oregon, it must qualify under the terms of the Oregon Business Corporation Act.

Businesses do not necessarily incorporate in the state in which they are located or in which they expect to transact the majority of their operations. Larger businesses often "shop around" for the state whose corporate laws are the most favorable. Many general business corporations choose Delaware or Nevada as a home state and qualify to do business in other states.

Delaware is particularly popular because of its hospitable statutes, which require the corporation to have a registered office within the state but do not require it to transact any actual business in Delaware. In addition, the Delaware Courts of Chancery offers litigants judges with experience and expertise in business law.

An **alien corporation** is one formed under the laws of a state or country other than one of the fifty United States, the District of Columbia, or the territories of Guam, Puerto Rico, or the U.S. Virgin Islands. A British or French corporation would be an alien corporation in the United States.

**Public or Private**

In addition, corporations are categorized as **public** or **private**. If shares are **publicly traded**, they are registered with the Securities and Exchange Commission and may be traded through a stock exchange or "over the counter."

A private corporation's shares are **privately held** and not publicly traded. One may purchase shares from a private corporation only by

- buying shares directly from the corporation with approval of the board of directors or

- buying shares from an existing shareholder – if the terms of the shareholders' agreement permit such a sale.

One might acquire the shares as a result of death or divorce, but the well-written shareholders' agreement addresses those contingencies as well.

**Creating the Corporation**

In many states the document of application for corporate existence is called the **articles of incorporation**. Other states – including Delaware, a popular choice of state for incorporation – call the document a **certificate of incorporation**. "Articles" is the more frequently used term. The generic term for the enabling document is "**charter**," based on the historic occurrence of states granting charters to business entities.

Whatever its name, the document must be filed to create the corporation. A corporation is "born" not when its founders discuss the prospect, nor when the incorporator sends the document to the appropriate filing agency (usually a secretary of state), but when the filing agency declares the corporation formed.

If a delayed filing date is desired and the statutes permit such a request, one may request a filing date at some point in the future – either on a specific date or when a specific event occurs. Such a delay is often limited to 90 days.

### Elements of the Articles of Incorporation

The requirements of articles of incorporation are set forth in the **enabling statute**. At a minimum articles usually contain:

- the name of the corporation

- the period of duration of the corporation (usually in perpetuity, as continuity of existence is one of the advantages of the corporate form of doing business)

- the purposes for which the corporation is organized, often stated very broadly so as not to restrict the corporation's future activities

- the number of shares the corporation is authorized to issue – including class or series, if any, and possibly the par value of each share (or a statement of no par value, a term that will be discussed in Chapter Twelve)

- the name of the registered agent, or agent for service of process, who will receive mail or service on behalf of the corporation

- the registered office, which is the address of the registered agent and may or may not be the address of the corporation's principal place of business and

- the name and address of each incorporator.

Some states also require

•     the number of initial directors, the name of each initial director, and his or her address and

•     a statement of minimum capitalization.

Often articles of incorporation will address other issues, which will be discussed in detail in Chapter Ten:

•     Will the shareholders have preemptive rights?

•     May the shareholders cumulate their votes when electing the board of directors?

•     May the shareholders take action through a written consent of the holders of the majority of shares entitled to vote on a question, or is the unanimous written consent of all shareholders entitled to vote on the question required?

Some states award these rights by default unless the rights are specifically denied. Other states require that the issue be addressed if such rights are to be claimed.

Articles may also address:

•     restriction on transfer of the shares
•     limited liability of a shareholder
•     limited liability of a director
•     indemnification of an agent of the corporation
•     whether amendment of the bylaws is restricted to shareholders (or whether the board of directors may amend the bylaws) or
•     what happens when a director has a conflict of interest.

"**Indemnification**" means that the corporation will financially support its agents by paying their legal fees and expenses if and when they are sued for some action they have undertaken solely because they were agents of the corporation.

Articles of incorporation may include any lawful provision. The more detailed provisions are not set forth in the articles because

- articles of incorporation are a matter of public record, and most persons prefer to keep business details confidential; and

- the only way to change articles of incorporation is to file formal articles of amendment, which involves a fee and time.

Most corporations prefer to put unique or confidential details in their bylaws or in the actions of the board of directors or shareholders. These are not filed on the public record and may be changed by an internal vote.

If the corporation is to be a close corporation, a professional corporation, or a nonprofit corporation, that information must be specified in the articles of incorporation. For example, the articles of incorporation of a nonprofit corporation may require a statement that the corporation is nonprofit.

## Requirements of Being an Incorporator

One need not pass a bar examination to act as an incorporator and create a corporation. One must, however,

- have achieved a certain age (in most states, 18);
- have enough money for the filing fee; and
- be able to string together language that is acceptable for filing under the statutes of the state of domestication.

The catch is deciding what language to string together. That is where competent legal advice is important. An attorney should know what language to insert and what to omit to suit a particular situation.

## What Does the Incorporator Do?

The incorporator signs and files the articles of incorporation. Depending on the business scenario, the incorporator may be the promoter of the new corporation, responsible for obtaining capital (funding) for the corporation.

Such funding is usually assured through **subscription agreements** – commitments by persons to purchase shares once the corporation is formed.

More often, the incorporator's duty is ministerial only: a "mere scrivener." In either case, upon filing of the articles of incorporation, all responsibility and authority pass to the director (s) named in the articles or subsequently named by the incorporator.

## Naming the Corporation

Most states require their domestic and foreign corporations to use certain words in a name, such as "Corporation" or "Incorporated." Alternatives are abbreviations: "Corp." or "Inc." Some states allow the use of the word "company" for either an unincorporated or incorporated entity, so the word "company" in a name is not a sure sign that an entity is incorporated.

The name must not be **deceptively similar** to a name already in use by another corporation, a limited partnership, or a limited liability company. "Deceptively similar" means the name might confuse the public into thinking the name represents another business.

## Forbidden Names

If a name has been reserved or registered by someone else, it cannot be used until the reservation or registration expires.

### *Registration*

You may register a name, often for the period of a year, without using the name. Registration keeps other people from using the name. This procedure is used by large businesses who do not plan to use the name in a certain state but do not want anyone using it in the meantime. It temporarily protects the name without having to register it as a trademark.

*Reservation*

A reservation indicates the intent to use the reserved name. A reservation implies

- an intent to incorporate or
- an intent to change the name of an existing entity or
- an intent to qualify to do business in the state under that name.

Some states accept name reservations by phone. To reserve a name in Delaware, for example, call the 900 number of the state's Department of Corporations. The reservation fee will be charged to the number from which you are calling, and a reservation number will be given you as evidence. The transaction is paperless. When the reservation expires, it may be renewed by phone.

Other states require an application in writing, accompanied by a fee. Most states accept faxed applications; some accept credit cards.

**The Name**

If an entity is already using a precise name or a name deceptively similar thereto, the applicant will not be able to reserve the name. Additionally, the name may not be available if there is a **similar name**. The secretary of state may state that the name is available only with a **letter of consent** from the entity using the similar name. (Note that "similar name" is not the same standard as "deceptively similar name," described above.)

**Utilizing the Name**

It is advisable to take action and reserve the name, or incorporate the corporation, before anyone else uses the name. How do you assemble articles of incorporation? Follow the applicable statutes.

But beware! You may need *more* in the articles than the basic information required by the statutes. Legal advice is a wise idea.

**The Corporation Comes Into Existence**

If the articles meet the legal requirements of the state statutes, a document is issued declaring that the corporation has come into existence. Some states call this document a **certificate of incorporation**.

The corporation is not "you" using another name. It is a separate, legal entity that can do any lawful business action that a natural person can do except physically pick up a pen and sign. The corporation can buy, sell, hire, fire, rent, lease, sue, be sued, loan, or borrow.

A common law theory called *ultra vires* holds that a corporation may not take actions exceeding its lawful purposes and powers. It is therefore customary to employ in the articles of incorporation language from the enabling statute that a corporation can take any action that is lawful under the laws of the state in which it has been incorporated.

**Important Terms**

Alien corporation
Articles of incorporation
Authorized shares
Capitalization
Certificate of authority
Certificate of incorporation
Corporate name
Corporation
Deceptively similar name
Domestic corporation

Foreign corporation
Letter of consent
Privately held corporation
Publicly traded corporation
Registered agent
Registered name
Reserved name
Similar name
*Ultra vires*

## Important Concepts

A corporation can be subcategorized as foreign, domestic, alien.

A corporation can be subcategorized as public or private.

To create a corporation, one must

- choose a name and obtain its use
- file articles of incorporation and
- capitalize the corporation.

# Chapter Ten

# CREATION OF THE CORPORATION, II

Articles of incorporation represent an agreement as to the operation of the corporation.

An enabling statute is the primary source of authority for the operation of the corporation. After the enabling statute, the articles of incorporation are the secondary source of authority. The bylaws are the third source of authority for operation.

## Name

If acceptable, the name will be precisely what is set forth in the first article. There can be no spelling errors.

## Duration

Stating a specific duration runs the risk of allowing the corporation's authority to transact business to expire. Thus, unlike the partnership form of business in which a specific term is preferred in order to prevent the creation of a partnership-at-will, there is no advantage in stating a specific duration for the corporation's existence.

## Purpose

A corporation for profit can be organized for any lawful purpose. An unlawful purpose does not mean that the purpose is illegal. It is simply a purpose not authorized by the statute, such as banking. The operation of a bank is provided for in statutes other than general corporation laws.

As pointed out in the previous chapter, language regarding the corporation's purpose is generally taken directly from the enabling statute's language: any and all purposes for which corporations may be incorporated in that state.

## Capitalization

The capitalization of a corporation represents the investment by its owners that enables the corporation to commence and continue operations. This investment is usually in the form of some sort of **consideration**, or value, that is exchanged for shares of the corporation's shares of stock as evidence of ownership of a portion of the corporation.

The consideration may be cash, assets of another organization, services rendered, physical equipment, abstract intellectual property, a promissory note – whatever the statute permits.

To prevent undercapitalization, a statute may require an affirmative statement that the corporation will not commence doing business until it has received a specific, minimum capitalization for the issuance of its shares.

## Authorized Shares

Authorized shares are the total number of shares that a corporation is permitted to issue. The **par value** and distribution of the shares among classes must be stated in the articles of incorporation. Par value denotes the minimum amount for which a share of stock may be sold. One cent is frequently used as par value.

If there is only one class of shares designated in the articles, that class is called **common**. A second class, if created, is called **preferred**.

The preferences, limitations, and relative rights of the shares of each class must be described in the articles of incorporation. Each class may have series within the class, as Series A or Series B.

## Denial of Preemptive Rights

A corporation may limit or deny its shareholders preemptive rights by including terms and conditions in the articles of incorporation. A

**preemptive right** is the right of first refusal to purchase more shares, triggered by the corporation's future issuance of shares.

If preemptive rights exist when the corporation issues additional shares, it must offer the shares to current shareholders for purchase so that the existing shareholders can maintain their proportion of ownership. Or the corporation may need to obtain from each existing shareholder a waiver of the shareholder's preemptive rights. If the shareholders decline to purchase the shares, the shares can then be offered for sale to others.

This polling process can be time-consuming and onerous, and most corporations avoid the issue by denying preemptive rights.

In some states (Delaware and Florida, for example), preemptive rights do not exist unless specifically stated in the articles of incorporation.

**Registered Agent and Registered Office**

The **registered agent** is the person who receives service of process, notice, or demand on behalf of the corporation. If a natural person, he or she may or may not be a director or officer of the corporation. A registered agent may be a statutory person. Many corporations name a service company as registered agent.

A corporation must continuously keep the state informed of its registered agent and the registered agent's address, called the **registered office**. Failure to do so could result in involuntary dissolution by the state for failure to comply with the enabling statute. A second serious possibility is not receiving notice of suits filed against the corporation, which could result in a default judgment in favor of the person serving the notice.

**Initial Board of Directors**

The enabling statute sets forth the minimum number of directors required for a domestic corporation. Even if the number is three, the statute may provide that a one-shareholder corporation may lawfully have only one director or a two-shareholder corporation may lawfully have only two directors.

## Other Things to Know About Filing Articles

The incorporator, or incorporators, must **execute** (sign) the articles. Many states accept a faxed or electronic signature. Indeed, a state may accept any faxed or electronic document for filing, so long as the filer has made provision for simultaneous payment of the filing fee.

If a " hard copy" (piece of paper with an original signature) is being presented, a state often wants the original and a photocopy of that original.

Some topics not addressed in articles are:

- names of the anticipated shareholders or investors
- names of the anticipated officers
- the corporation's assumed name, if any, or
- whether the corporation intends to elect Subchapter S status.

### Important Terms

| | |
|---|---|
| Common stock | Preferred stock |
| Consideration | Registered agent |
| Par value | Series of shares |
| Preemptive rights | |

### Important Concept

Each state has certain items of information that are statutorily required to be included in its articles of incorporation.

---

# Chapter Eleven

# GETTING UNDERWAY

---

An organizational meeting must be held by the corporation soon after the certificate of incorporation is issued. The primary purposes of this meeting are to adopt bylaws, elect officers, and issue shares of stock.

In lieu of such a meeting, the directors can – and generally do – give their unanimous written consent to resolutions that would have been adopted had a meeting been held. Because these are generally standard "housekeeping" resolutions that generate no controversy, it is standard practice to prepare a unanimous written consent in lieu of actually holding an organizational meeting.

See Appendix I for a chart listing the authorizing statute in each state that permits directors to conduct business by unanimous written consent in lieu of meeting.

Examples of the "housekeeping" items to be covered in the organizational meeting are:

1. *Articles of incorporation.* The directors approve, accept, ratify, and adopt the already-filed articles as the articles of the corporation. The secretary of the corporation is directed to insert in the minute book the file-stamped articles of incorporation and the certificate that has been issued to the corporation by the secretary of state.

2. *Bylaws.* The directors approve and adopt the bylaws and direct the secretary to insert a copy in the minute book. Bylaws regulate how the corporation is operated. They may include:

    a. Offices.
        Registered office and registered agent
        Other offices within or without the state of domesticity

b.       Shareholders.
         Meetings
                    (i)      annual
                    (ii)     special
                    (iii)    place of
                    (iv)     notice of
         Voting
                    (i)      list of voting shareholders
                    (ii)     voting of shares
                    (iii)    method of voting
                    (iv)     use of proxies
         Quorum
                    (i)      What constitutes
                    (ii)     How withdrawn
         Closing transfer records and choosing record date
         Action without a meeting

c.       Directors.
         Management responsibilities
         Number and changes in number
         Election
         Term
         Removal
         Qualifications
         Vacancies
         Meetings
                    (i)      Place of
                    (ii)     First or organizational
                    (iii)    Regular
                    (iv)     Special, notice thereof
         Quorum: what constitutes
         Majority vote: what constitutes
                    (i)      simple?
                    (ii)     two-thirds?
                    (iii)    three-fourths?
         Procedures, minutes
         Presumption of assent

Compensation, if any
Action without a meeting

d.      Committees of the board.
Designation, number, qualifications, term, authority
Meetings: regular, special
Quorum: what constitutes
Majority vote: what constitutes
Procedures, minutes
Compensation, if any
Responsibilities and limits thereon

e.      Meetings, generally.
What constitutes proper notice
Waiver of notice
Telephonic or similar meetings

f.      Officers and other agents.
Number
Titles
Election of
Term
Qualifications
Removal
Vacancies
Authority
Compensation, if any
Duties

        (i)      Chairperson of the Board
        (ii)     President
        (iii)    Vice Presidents, if any
        (iv)    Secretary
        (v)     Assistant Secretaries, if any
        (vi)    Treasurer, if any
        (vii)   Assistant Treasurers, if any

g.      Share certificates.
Shares, certificated or uncertificated

                Issuance, consideration therefor
                Lost, stolen or destroyed certificates
                Transfer of shares
                Registration of shareholders
                Legends

h.       Miscellaneous.
                Dividends
                Books and records
                Fiscal year
                Seal
                Requirement for attestation by secretary
                Invalid provisions, should question arise, and use of
                 headings in the table of contents
                Procedure for amending

       3.     *Minute book.* The directors approve and adopt the minute book and direct the secretary to retain custody of the minute book and to keep it current by inserting therein (i) the minutes of meetings of the shareholders, the directors, or any committees and (ii) any written consents given in lieu of meetings. A minute book usually has these sections:

a.       Charter
                Original articles of incorporation
                Original amendments thereto
                Any documents filed with government agencies

b.       First meeting – minutes or consent in lieu thereof

c.       Minutes, or consents in lieu thereof, of meetings of
                    Shareholders
                      Directors
                      Committees of the board of directors

d.       Bylaws

e.       Share records

4.     *Seal*. If a corporate seal has been ordered, the directors approve and adopt the seal. They also provide that the use of a seal will not be required to validate any instrument issued or executed by the corporation. Not all states require a corporate seal, but the use of one is customary, particularly in real estate transactions.

5.     *Share certificates*. The directors approve and adopt the form of certificate that will reflect ownership of shares of stock of the corporation. They then direct the secretary to insert a specimen of each approved certificate in the minute book. A book of preprinted certificates ordered with the minute book will usually include a nonnumbered certificate stamped " SPECIMEN" across its face. This specimen may either be removed and placed behind the consent or simply left in the front of the share record book for ready reference.

6.     *Number of directors*. By this organizational consent, the directors decide how many members the board will have: one, three, five, or more. It is not required that a board have an odd number of directors, but doing so avoids deadlock votes. The phrase " until further action by the board of directors or the shareholders of the corporation" should be included in this resolution so the number of board members can be changed from time to time.

7.     *Election of officers*. The laws under which the corporation was formed will specify the required officers and their required titles, if any. In many cases one person may hold all of the offices. If the corporation wants more officers than the required ones, it may so elect. Each officer serves until a successor is elected or appointed and qualified or until the officer dies, resigns, or is removed from office by the directors.

8.     *Compensation of officers*. If the officers are to be paid for serving, the compensation is set forth here. If they are not to be compensated, a phrase such as the following is used:

RESOLVED, that until further action by the board of directors of the Corporation, the officers of the

Corporation shall serve as such without salary or other compensation.

9.     *Issuance of shares of stock.* At this point the directors approve issuing shares of stock to the persons who wish to become shareholders in the corporation. The following is sample language:

> RESOLVED, that the Corporation issue an aggregate of [number of shares, either in words or digits] of its [common/preferred] [class of stock, if applicable] [series of stock, if applicable], $[amount of par value] per share, to [name of shareholder] in exchange for and against receipt by the Corporation of $[amount of consideration] as consideration therefor.

The directors then authorize the "proper officers" of the corporation (the people they have just elected) to issue a certificate or certificates representing the shares.

The directors further state that the shares shall be "duly authorized, validly issued, fully paid and nonassessable."

In other words, the shares are authorized by the corporation, issued at the direction of the corporation, fully paid for by the consideration stated, and not subject to further assessment after the consideration has been paid.

10.     *Election as a Subchapter S corporation.* If the corporation qualifies as a Subchapter S corporation, and if the shareholders so choose, this is the place to memorialize election of such tax status.

Including the election in the written consent is, however, not sufficient to cause it to happen. IRS Form 2553 must be completed and filed. See Chapter Fourteen for a discussion of Subchapter S status.

11.     *Banking.* The corporation will probably want to open one or more bank accounts and possibly borrow money. The corporation

can authorize the president, the treasurer, or any officer to borrow funds, as needed, for the corporation and to acknowledge the existence of formal banking resolutions that a bank will ask the corporation to execute.

Including language as " such resolutions shall be deemed to be copied in the minute book as if set forth therein in full" will avoid stuffing the minute book with copies of standard banking resolutions every time the corporation opens an account or takes out a loan.

12.     *Annual meeting of shareholders.* The shareholders must meet annually or give a written consent in lieu of the annual meeting. The date of the meeting may be specific, as to " the fourth Monday of May unless such fourth Monday shall fall on a legal holiday, in which case . . ." or broad, permitting the board of directors to schedule the annual meeting of the shareholders. Sample language for a broad resolution is:

RESOLVED, that the annual meeting of shareholders of the Corporation shall be held during each calendar year on such date and at such time as shall be designated from time to time by the board of directors.

13.     *Organizational expenses.* The corporation may allow organizational expenses to be taken out of consideration. The directors may authorize the " appropriate officer" (usually the treasurer) to pay charges and expenses incident to the organization of the corporation and to reimburse persons who incurred expenses.

14.     *Fiscal year.* The directors set the fiscal year to end on the last day of a month of their choice. Most business entities end a fiscal year on the quarter in March, June, September, or December, with the latter most common.

15.     *Authorization to do business in other states.* The directors may authorize the " appropriate officers" to qualify the

corporation in foreign jurisdictions where it owns property or conducts business.

While this authorization could be given on a state-by-state basis as the business develops, including this "blanket" language in the organizational consent will prevent the necessary authorization being overlooked in future.

16.    *General authorization*. The directors give the officers a general authorization to do what must be done to get the corporation going. Often, the directors also ratify actions that may have already been taken by using language such as this:

> RESOLVED, that any and all action taken by any proper officer of the Corporation prior to the date this consent is actually executed in effecting the purposes of the foregoing resolutions is hereby ratified, approved, confirmed, and adopted in all respects.

17.    *Specific authorization*. The directors may wish to approve specific agreements into which the corporation is entering, such as leases, purchase contracts or employment agreements.

The consent concludes with a paragraph stating that the persons executing the written consent are doing so as of the date "first above written," which will be the date inserted at the top of the first page. Unless there is a compelling reason to do otherwise, the bylaws, the written consent in lieu of organizational meeting, and the initial share certificates are given the effective date on which the corporation was formed.

Each director must sign the consent. If that is impractical, they may sign in "**multiple counterparts**," meaning that each director signs a different page of paper and all the pages are put into the minute book. This is usually done when the directors live in different cities or when there are so many directors that it would take too long to circulate one page among all of them.

## Important Terms

Authorization
Bylaws
Charter
Corporate seal
Electing officers
Execution
Fiscal year

Issuing shares
Minute book
Multiple counterparts
Resolutions
Specimen certificate
Unanimous consent in lieu of
meeting

## Important Concepts

The initial board of directors must hold an organizational meeting or give a written consent in lieu thereof.

At the organizational meeting (or by such consent), the directors attend to "housekeeping" duties to get the corporation underway, including electing officers, adopting bylaws, and issuing shares of stock.

# Chapter Twelve

# SHAREHOLDERS AND SHARES

Shareholders own the corporation in proportion to their ownership of the shares of stock issued by the corporation. For example, if a corporation issues one thousand shares of stock, the owner of one hundred shares owns ten percent of the corporation.

**Types of Shares**

There are two basic types of shares: **common** and **preferred**.

The default type is common. If only one type of shares is authorized, those shares are common even if the term is not specifically used in the charter document.

The articles may provide for "**blank check preferred**" stock. "Blank check" is a colloquial term meaning that the board of directors has been given the authority to set, at some future date, the specific rights and privileges to be enjoyed by holders of preferred shares. Often these rights and privileges result from negotiations that induce investors to invest in the corporation, thus they are not known when the original articles of incorporation are filed.

When the definite terms that apply to preferred shares have been reached, that information is filed with the state agency in a document having a title such as "Statement of Rights and Privileges." The statement is not regarded as an amendment to the articles of incorporation, but as a clarification of the "blank check" provision in the original articles.

**Dividends**

Unless restricted by the articles or the bylaws, shareholders of both types of shares have a right to receive dividends, to vote upon questions that come before the corporation, and to receive property upon the corporation's liquidation.

**Dividends** are a portion of the corporation's profits that are paid to its shareholders on a *pro rata* basis. Dividends are authorized and declared by the board of directors. The funds used to pay the dividends must be from current net profits or earned surplus. Use of other funds may impair the capitalization of the corporation and subject the directors to personal liability for improper distributions.

Dividends are paid from earnings, not capital. Unless there are net earnings, shareholders have no right to dividends. Dividends vary in size with the profitability of the corporation, and they will not be paid at all if the corporation is not operating at a profit. Even if the corporation is operating at a profit, the board of directors may decide it is in the corporation's best interests to reinvest the money in the corporation rather than use it to pay dividends to the shareholders.

As the name suggests, shareholders of preferred stock receive preferential treatment. Preferred shares have preference over any other class of stock regarding the payment of dividends during the life of the corporation and with respect to assets upon liquidation.

Dividends on preferred shares may be noncumulative, cumulative, or partially cumulative.

Holders of **noncumulative preferred shares** receive dividends only if the board declares them. If a dividend is not declared, the amount does not accumulate for payment in future years.

Unpaid dividends on **cumulative preferred shares**, however, accumulate for payment in future years.

**Partially cumulative shares** combine the other two forms.

## Share Certificates

In most privately held corporations, ownership of stock is evidenced by **share certificates** or, as they are more commonly called, **stock certificates**. Although the enabling statute may provide for **uncertificated shares**, the common practice in privately held corporations is to create certificates and deliver them to the shareholders.

Shares of stock are considered personal property. It is important to remember that the shares, which are abstract, are the items of value. The pieces of paper called certificates only represent or memorialize the abstract shares.

Shareholders have a general right to transfer their shares of stock. This right is called the **right of alienation**. Transferability of shares can, however, be restricted by the articles, bylaws, or a shareholders' agreement.

Any restriction on the transferability of the shares must be noted conspicuously on the share certificate representing the shares, or the restriction may not be enforceable.

The applicable statute may require a certain size of font or bold lettering on the certificate that reads, for example:

> Transfer of the shares represented by this certificate is in some manner restricted. See reverse hereof for details on such restrictions.

Or

> See reverse hereof for certain legended information on restrictions on transferability of the shares represented by this certificate.

## Legends

The term "legended information" refers to a series of paragraphs known as **legends**. Each legend sets forth some restriction on transferring the shares represented by the certificate.

Following are some sample legends. Unless the statute prescribes specific language for a legend, the entity creating the certificate may choose its own words.

### 1933 Legend

If the shares have not been registered with any federal or state securities agency, the "**1933 legend**" may be affixed. This commonly used legend gets its colloquial name from the Securities Act of 1933.

> THE SHARES REPRESENTED BY THIS
> CERTIFICATE HAVE NOT BEEN REGISTERED
> UNDER THE SECURITIES ACT OF 1933, AS
> AMENDED, OR ANY STATE SECURITIES LAWS,
> AND MAY NOT BE SOLD, TRANSFERRED, OR
> OTHERWISE DISPOSED OF WITHOUT SUCH
> REGISTRATION OR THE AVAILABILITY OF AN
> EXEMPTION FROM REGISTRATION UNDER
> FEDERAL AND ALL APPLICABLE STATE
> SECURITIES LAWS.

This is a "buyer beware" clause, reminding a prospective shareholder that the corporation is not required to, and does not intend to, have its shares reviewed by any federal or state securities agency. Further, warns this legend, it may be difficult or impossible in the future to sell the shares without obtaining an exemption under federal or state securities laws.

### Denial of preemptive rights legend

If the enabling statute permits preemptive rights but these rights have been denied in the articles of incorporation, a legend notifying the public of that fact must be set forth on the certificate representing those shares without preemptive rights.

> NO SHAREHOLDER OF THE CORPORATION OR ANY OTHER PERSON SHALL HAVE ANY PREEMPTIVE RIGHT TO PURCHASE OR SUBSCRIBE TO ANY SHARES OR ANY OTHER SECURITIES OF THE CORPORATION NOW OR HEREAFTER AUTHORIZED. A FULL STATEMENT OF THE DENIAL OF ANY PREEMPTIVE RIGHTS IS SET FORTH IN THE ARTICLES OF INCORPORATION OF THE CORPORATION ON FILE WITH THE SECRETARY OF STATE OF [state], A COPY OF WHICH WILL BE FURNISHED TO THE RECORD HOLDER OF THIS CERTIFICATE WITHOUT CHARGE ON WRITTEN REQUEST TO THE CORPORATION AT ITS PRINCIPAL OFFICE.

*Preferred shares authorized legend*

A holder of preferred shares knows that the corporation is authorized to issue common shares, because common is the default type of share. It is possible, however, that a prospective purchaser of common shares could be unaware that preferred shares are authorized.

A state may, therefore, require that a notice be placed upon certificates representing shares of common stock.

> THIS CORPORATION IS AUTHORIZED TO ISSUE SHARES OF MORE THAN ONE CLASS AND TO ISSUE PREFERRED SHARES IN SERIES. A STATEMENT OF THE DESIGNATIONS, PREFERENCES, LIMITATIONS AND RELATIVE RIGHTS OF THE SHARES OF EACH CLASS AUTHORIZED TO BE ISSUED BY THE CORPORATION, THE VARIATIONS IN THE RELATIVE RIGHTS AND PREFERENCES OF THE SHARES OF EACH SERIES OF PREFERRED

SHARES (TO THE EXTENT THEY HAVE BEEN
FIXED AND DETERMINED), AND THE
AUTHORITY OF THE BOARD OF DIRECTORS OF
THE CORPORATION TO FIX AND DETERMINE
THE RELATIVE RIGHTS AND PREFERENCES OF
ANY SERIES OF PREFERRED SHARES ARE SET
FORTH IN THE ARTICLES OF INCORPORATION
OF THE CORPORATION ON FILE IN THE OFFICE
OF THE SECRETARY OF STATE OF [state]. THE
CORPORATION WILL FURNISH A COPY OF SUCH
STATEMENT TO THE RECORD HOLDER OF THIS
CERTIFICATE WITHOUT CHARGE ON WRITTEN
REQUEST TO THE CORPORATION AT ITS
PRINCIPAL PLACE OF BUSINESS.

*Shareholders' agreement legend*

If the transfer of shares is controlled by a shareholders' agreement,
whether the corporation is a close corporation or not, a legend must be
set forth on the certificates representing the controlled shares.

THE SHARES OF STOCK REPRESENTED BY THIS
CERTIFICATE ARE SUBJECT TO THE TERMS OF
A SHAREHOLDERS' AGREEMENT DATED
[effective date], BY AND AMONG THE
CORPORATION AND ITS SHAREHOLDERS,
WHICH AGREEMENT CONTAINS, AMONG
OTHER PROVISIONS, RESTRICTIONS ON THE
SALE, TRANSFER OR OTHER DISPOSITION, OR
THE REGISTRATION OR TRANSFER, OF THE
SHARES OF STOCK REPRESENTED BY THIS
CERTIFICATE. THE CORPORATION WILL
FURNISH A COPY OF SUCH AGREEMENT TO THE
RECORD HOLDER OF THIS CERTIFICATE
WITHOUT CHARGE ON WRITTEN REQUEST TO
THE CORPORATION AT ITS PRINCIPAL PLACE
OF BUSINESS.

## Voting agreement legend

If two or more shareholders have entered into an agreement that they will vote their shares as a block, this agreement must be memorialized in writing and presented to the corporation. Other shareholders are entitled to be aware of the voting agreement. Anyone purchasing the shares would also be a party to the voting agreement, so the certificates representing such controlled shares must bear a legend telling of the existence of such voting agreement. This voting agreement is sometimes called a pooling agreement.

> THE SHARES OF STOCK REPRESENTED BY THIS
> CERTIFICATE ARE SUBJECT TO THE TERMS OF
> A VOTING AGREEMENT DATED [effective date],
> BY AND AMONG CERTAIN SHAREHOLDERS OF
> THE CORPORATION. THE CORPORATION WILL
> FURNISH A COPY OF SUCH AGREEMENT TO THE
> RECORD HOLDER OF THIS CERTIFICATE
> WITHOUT CHARGE ON WRITTEN REQUEST TO
> THE CORPORATION AT ITS PRINCIPAL PLACE
> OF BUSINESS.

## Voting trust legend

If any shareholder has given his, her, or its right to vote to a trustee of a trust, certificates representing these shares must bear a legend telling of the existence of the trust and voting power of the trustee.

> THE SHARES OF STOCK REPRESENTED BY THIS
> CERTIFICATE ARE SUBJECT TO THE TERMS OF
> A VOTING TRUST DATED [effective date]. THE
> CORPORATION WILL FURNISH A COPY OF SUCH
> TRUST INSTRUMENT TO THE RECORD HOLDER
> OF THIS CERTIFICATE WITHOUT CHARGE ON
> WRITTEN REQUEST TO THE CORPORATION AT
> ITS PRINCIPAL PLACE OF BUSINESS.

*Irrevocable proxy legend*

If any shareholder has given an irrevocable proxy authorizing the proxy holder to vote the shares, certificates representing these shares must bear a legend telling of the existence of the proxy and rights of the proxy holder.

> THE SHARES OF STOCK REPRESENTED BY THIS
> CERTIFICATE ARE SUBJECT TO THE TERMS OF
> AN IRREVOCABLE PROXY DATED [effective date].
> THE CORPORATION WILL FURNISH A COPY OF
> SUCH PROXY TO THE RECORD HOLDER OF THIS
> CERTIFICATE WITHOUT CHARGE ON WRITTEN
> REQUEST TO THE CORPORATION AT ITS
> PRINCIPAL PLACE OF BUSINESS.

## Meetings of Shareholders

Bylaws provide the time and place for the **annual meeting** of shareholders. At this meeting, in addition to conducting business matters of the corporation, shareholders elect the board of directors.

If the annual meeting is not held within a certain time period (usually 13 months), the shareholders can petition the court to order that a meeting be held. The corporation does not dissolve, however, if the annual meeting is not held.

In addition to the annual meeting, **special meetings** of the shareholders may be called by the board of directors, specific officers, or a certain percentage of the shareholders, as authorized by the articles of incorporation or bylaws. The statute gives shareholders who own a certain percentage of shares the right to demand a meeting.

If the statute mandates, prior written notice of a special meeting must be provided to the shareholders, and only business described in the notice may be conducted at the meeting. At the special meeting, shareholders vote on corporate matters and transactions that require their approval.

A quorum of shareholders must be present in person or by proxy to conduct business at the meeting. Unless provided otherwise, a majority of the holders of the shares entitled to vote constitutes a **quorum**. A quorum is required in order to prevent significant corporate decisions from being made by a minority of the shareholders.

**Minutes**, which constitute a record of the meetings, must be kept, with a copy placed in the minute book.

### Action by Written Consent in Lieu of Meeting

Each state permits shareholders to dispense with a meeting and, if all agree, act instead by unanimous written consent. Some states, moreover, permit action by written consent of some, but not all, of the shareholders – a significant difference!

Suppose, for example, that one lone hold-out refuses to sign a consent intended to be unanimous. That one shareholder can force the others to call a meeting and take a formal vote in order to adopt the resolutions in the written consent. Because most states require a minimum notice of a shareholders meeting (usually ten days, the number of days used by the Model Business Corporation Act), the dissenting shareholder has time to try to bring others to his or her position.

Suppose, in a second example, that you own 51% of the issued shares of a corporation. You will always carry the question at any meeting when a vote is taken. Is it not more efficient to provide that you may sign a written consent and simply notify the holders of the other 49% of shares what action you have taken? Do you want to have to collect the signature of every other shareholder, risking that some shareholder will delay you as described in the previous example?

These examples illustrate the importance of choosing whether to require unanimous written consent in lieu of a shareholders' meeting or the written consent of fewer than all of the shareholders in lieu of a shareholders' meeting.

Once that choice has been made, there are two ways to reach the goal.

As of the publication date of this book, ten states had in their statutes as a *default* action in lieu of a meeting by the written consent of less than all shareholders. (Consult the chart in the appendices for details on these states and the percentages required.) In these ten states, to require unanimous consent of the shareholders in lieu of a meeting, specific language must be included in the articles of incorporation.

Nine states, in absolute mirror image, have as their default the unanimous written consent of shareholders *but permit* action by fewer shareholders *if* provided in the articles of incorporation.

The remaining states require unanimous consent only, with no variations. Consult the appendices to find your state's position as of the date of publication. (Remember that a legislature can, and will, amend statutes.)

**Voting**

*For the Board of Directors*

There are two types of voting: **straight** and **cumulative**. The articles of incorporation will control whether voting for the directors is straight or cumulative.

In straight voting, one share is entitled to one vote. In cumulative voting, each voting share is entitled to one vote for each director to be elected.

For example: if there are four directors to be elected, and a shareholder owns 50 shares, cumulative voting would give the shareholder 200 votes. The shareholder could vote all 200 for one director or spread the votes out among the four openings.

The purpose of cumulative voting is to enable minority shareholders to elect at least one director. If a shareholder entitled to cumulative voting decides to use that method, the shareholder must give prior written notice to the corporation's secretary, which triggers the right of the other shareholders to cumulate their votes as well.

*Other Voting*

Under ordinary circumstances, only holders of voting shares are entitled to vote on questions brought before the shareholders. In some instances, however, the question may be of such import that the statute mandates that all shareholders, even those holding nonvoting shares, may vote. Examples of such questions are dissolution of the corporation or the sale of all or substantially all of the corporation's assets.

**Voting Methods**

Shareholders can vote straight or cumulatively by several methods:

- in person
- by proxy
- by a voting trust
- by a voting agreement

*Proxy*

When a shareholder votes by **proxy** the shareholder has, before the shareholders' meeting, appointed another individual to vote in the shareholder's place. A proxy can take the form of an e-mail, telex, fax, or other transmission or reproduction of a writing executed by the shareholder.

Unless otherwise provided, the standard proxy expires in eleven months from the date of its execution This prevents a proxy from being used for more than one annual meeting unless specifically stated by the shareholder.

A proxy is revocable unless the proxy is **coupled with an interest** and the proxy form conspicuously states that it is irrevocable. A proxy is coupled with an interest if the proxyholder has some right of claim to the proxy. For example, the proxyholder may have purchased or agreed to purchase the shares represented by the proxy. An irrevocable proxy can be enforced by its holder.

*The Voting Trust*

Shareholders can also confer their right to vote upon a trustee by transferring their shares to the trustee via a **voting trust**. The trust agreement must be in writing, must be filed with the corporation, and is valid for a certain, stated period (often, no longer than ten years).

*The Voting Agreement*

Shareholders who vote by a **voting agreement**, however, are not required to transfer legal title of their shares to another. In a voting agreement the shareholders agree to pool their shares and vote as a unit to maximize the impact of their votes. The voting, or pooling, agreement must be in writing, must be filed with the corporation, and is valid for a stated period.

As noted above, any certificate representing shares controlled by a voting trust or a voting agreement must display a legend that the shares are subject to the provisions of the trust or agreement.

**Duties and Liabilities of Shareholders**

One of the fundamental advantages that entices persons to opt for the corporate business form is limited personal liability. Shareholders, officers, and directors are insulated from personal liability for debts of the corporation or torts committed by employees.

Shareholders have no liability for corporate debts and obligations once full consideration has been paid for the issuance of their shares. Thus, the shareholder's risk is limited to the amount of the shareholder's investment.

There are some narrowly construed exceptions to the rule of limited liability. These exceptions involve, for example:

- watered stock
- alter ego theory
- share subscriptions
- improper distributions

*Watered Stock*

Shares may have either a par value or a no par value. **Par value** shares have a specific minimum dollar value for which they must be sold, although it can be one cent or a fraction thereof. Some states do not even use the idea of par value. **No par value** or **stated value** shares are sold for an amount set periodically by the board.

Shares cannot be issued until they are paid for in full. **Watered stock** means that shares have been issued for property or services that are overvalued. The value of the shares has been diluted or "watered down." Full consideration has not been paid, and the shareholder is liable for the difference.

*The Alter Ego Theory*

A shareholder can also be held personally liable under the **alter ego theory**. In other words, if the corporation is found to be nothing but the "alter ego" of the owner, the owner will be denied the protection of limited personal liability. This theory disregards the legal fiction of the corporate entity's existence and is referred to as "**piercing the corporate veil**."

Not observing corporate formalities by failing to keep corporate affairs, assets, and transactions separate from personal ones is the primary reason for which a court can pierce the corporate veil.

A court can also pierce the corporate veil for undercapitalization or fraud that is likely to deceive creditors of the corporation into thinking that the corporation has greater assets than it actually does. The availability of the alter ego theory to pierce the corporate veil is a deterrent to such abuses.

*Share Subscription*

Another exception to the general rule of no personal liability for shareholders results from the contractual obligation they incur under a share subscription. A **share subscription** is a written agreement in which a commitment is made to purchase and pay for a specified number of unissued shares. A shareholder who fails to purchase and pay for the contracted shares has breached the agreement, and the corporation can sue to collect the amount owing for the unpurchased shares.

*Improper Distributions*

Shareholders are also personally liable for **improper distributions** of corporate profits through dividends. They are only liable for the amount received, however, if they knew the distribution was illegal.

## Important Terms

| | |
|---|---|
| Alter ego | Right of alienation |
| Annual meeting | Share certificates |
| Common stock | Shareholders |
| Cumulative voting | Special meeting |
| Dividend | Stated value |
| Noncumulative preferred shares | Share subscription |
| Par value | Straight voting |
| Pierce the corporate veil | Voting trust |
| Preferred stock | Voting agreement |
| Proxy | Watered stock |
| Quorum | Written consent in lieu of meeting |

## Important Concepts

Shareholders own the corporation through common or preferred shares of stock.

Shareholders elect the board of directors who, in turn, elect the officers.

Shareholders hold an annual meeting to elect the board of directors and conduct other business brought before them.

The alter ego theory allows a court to pierce the corporate veil and hold shareholders personally liable for certain acts.

Statutes control whether shareholders are permitted to act in lieu of a meeting only by unanimous written consent.

# Chapter Thirteen

# DIRECTORS AND OFFICERS

The initial board of directors is named by the incorporator, and thereafter directors are elected by the shareholders.

## Duties of a Director

The primary business conducted by the board of directors is making policy, declaring dividends, and electing officers.

## Term of a Director

Unless a director is removed, or the director dies or resigns, a director holds his or her seat on the board until the next annual shareholders' meeting (or a written consent given in lieu of the meeting), or until his or her successor has been elected or qualified.

Bylaws provide the mechanics for electing someone to fill a vacancy on the board of directors. Shareholders may always take this action, but, because the board meets more frequently than the shareholders, it is more efficient to provide that the remaining directors may fill vacancies. The person so appointed serves until the next meeting of shareholders, at which time the shareholders may (or may not) confirm the interim appointment by electing the replacement to a full term in his or her own right.

If the bylaws provide for directors to be **classified** (divided into groups whose terms end in different years), there will be a specific number elected each year. The membership of the board will change annually as a result of this classification. Classification serves other purposes: it brings new persons with fresh ideas to the board, and it gives directors a definite number of years in which to accomplish their goals for the corporation.

To avoid a voting deadlock, a board often has an odd number of directors.

## Qualifications of a Director

Usually a director need not be a shareholder or a resident of the corporation's state of domesticity. An **"inside director"** will be an employee of the corporation, such as an executive. An **"outside director"** is someone who is invited to join the board based on his or her expertise or prestige in a certain field.

Directors owe the corporation the duty of **loyalty**. They cannot engage in self-dealing. Directors must always consider the best interest of the corporation and its shareholders. It is therefore imperative that the director be attentive to the facts and circumstances of transactions into which the corporation enters.

## Meetings

Directors hold annual and special meetings, as do shareholders. The directors' annual meeting is generally held immediately after the shareholders' annual meeting at which those directors were elected.

The bylaws prescribe the method and manner of required notice, if any, to directors for the meeting. Attendance by a director at a meeting is a waiver of notice of that meeting. A director can, however, attend the meeting without waiving notice if he or she attends solely to contest the notice or the business to be transacted at the meeting.

As with shareholders, a majority of the directors must be present at the meeting to form the quorum necessary to transact business. The articles or bylaws may increase the number of directors constituting a quorum.

Unless he or she dissents for the record, a director who attends a meeting is presumed to have assented to any action taken by the board at that meeting.

## Officers

Officers manage the day-to-day operations of the corporation.

Statutes may require a corporation to have a certain number of officers, one of whom is designated keeper of the corporation's records. California, for example, specifies a president, a secretary, and a chief financial officer (called a treasurer in most states).

In a business corporation, it is common for two or more offices to be held by the same person. Statutes of nonprofit corporations generally forbid one person from holding multiple offices.

All officers are agents of the corporation and serve at the pleasure of the board of directors. Their authority is prescribed by the articles, bylaws, and actions of the board of directors. Thus, officers' authority is subject to the theory of agency.

## Duties of Directors and Officers

As with directors, officers owe the corporation the duty of loyalty.

The duty of care requires both directions and officers to make reasonable inquiries into the transactions of the corporation. In exercising this role, directors and officers enjoy the protection of the **business judgment rule**.

This rule creates a presumption that the director or officer acted with care. It protects a director or officer in all but extreme cases such as gross negligence or willful conduct. The burden of proof is on the person attacking the action of the directors or the officers.

In addition, the enabling statute may limit the liability of directors who have acted in good faith, been diligent in their duties, and treated the corporation's assets with the same standard of care they treat their own. If a director has faithfully attended meetings and relied upon the advice of attorneys and accountants in making decisions to the best of the director's ability, he or she is not likely to be held personally liable.

Nevertheless, in today's litigious society, many corporations routinely carry **director and officer (d&o) liability insurance** to fund the defense if the directors and officers are sued in the course of carrying out their duties.

## Liabilities of Directors and Officers

*Bases for Liability*

Directors and officers owe fiduciary duties to the corporation and its shareholders. Fiduciary duties are defined pursuant to agency law and include due care, loyalty, and obedience. Failure to comply with these duties can subject the director or officer to personal liability.

Additional liabilities are imposed on the director or officer by statute. For example: directors who allow distributions when there is insufficient earned surplus are **jointly and severally liable** to the corporation for the amount by which the distributed amount exceeds the authorized amount, if any. This means that the amount of the excess payment can be recovered from any one or all of the directors.

Directors escape personal liability, however, if they relied on certain information when making a distribution. As mentioned above, this information includes written opinions of the corporation's legal counsel and financial statements prepared by professional accountants. The attorney and the accountants, however, can be held personally liable for negligence or fraudulent acts that might have misled the directors.

*Attention to Transactions*

Unless he or she dissents for the record, a director who attends a meeting is presumed to have assented to any action taken by the board at the meeting. It is imperative, therefore, that the director be attentive to the facts and circumstances of transactions into which the corporation enters.

This requirement is true for the officers. Their duty of care requires both directors and officers to make reasonable inquiries into the transactions of the corporation. In exercising this role, officers and directors enjoy the protection of the aforementioned business judgment rule.

A transaction that appears to be self-dealing due to a conflict of interest of the director or officer, but is otherwise fair or approved by the other directors and shareholders following disclosure of the conflict of interest, is not void or voidable for that reason alone.

The disinterested approval and inherent fairness of the transaction can demonstrate that the director or officer did not breach the duty of loyalty.

### Derivative Action Shareholder Suits

Shareholders can bring a suit on behalf of the corporation to challenge actions of the board and management that the shareholders believe have harmed the corporation.

Generally, before bringing this type of suit, shareholders must first approach the board for corrective action of management. But if the suit is against the board of directors, there is a conflict of interest in the corrective request. These suits are called **derivative actions** because the shareholders' cause of action is derived from the corporation and any recovery will go to the corporation, not the shareholders personally.

### The Business Opportunity Rule

The **business opportunity rule** (sometimes called the corporate opportunity rule) requires disclosure of material facts that affect the operation of the corporation.

Enabling statutes often deal with the issue of an **interested director**, meaning a board member who may profit from some action of the board. The statute may require the interested director to disclose his or her interest and potential conflict to the other directors. After such disclosure, however, the interested director is not prohibited from voting upon the question. The key is voluntary disclosure.

**Liability under Contract or Tort Law**

In addition to the previously-stated theories and statutes, directors and officers can be held personally liable to third parties under contract and tort law. Agency theory applies.

Directors and officers who act as agents of the corporation can be held personally liable for contracts into which they enter with a third party if they fail to disclose that they are acting for the corporation. To prevent liability, a director or an officer should tell the third party that he or she is contracting on behalf of and for the corporation. For a fuller discussion of this topic, see the authors' *Introduction to Contracts*.

Tort (civil wrong) liability can be imposed on a director or an officer who authorized, directed, or otherwise participated in the tort. For example, an executive who knowingly authorized the manufacture of a defective product could be held personally liable for damages caused by the product even if he or she did not assist in its actual production or distribution. Case law abounds with tort lawsuits in which the board members were named as defendants.

**Statutory Liability**

Various statutes also create personal contractual and tort liability. The following is only a sampling of these statutes:

- Clean Air Act
- Toxic Substances Control Act
- Employee Retirement Income Security Act (ERISA)
- Securities Act of 1933
- Securities and Exchange Act of 1934

*Environmental Statutes*

The Clean Air Act and Toxic Substances Control Act impose civil and criminal liabilities on corporate officials who participate in or know of their corporation's violations of these federal environmental statutes.

*Securities Statutes*

The Securities Act of 1933 (the " 1933 Act" ) and the Securities and Exchange Act of 1934 (the " 1934 Act" ) impose personal liability on officers and directors for securities fraud.

The 1933 Act is a disclosure statute and covers the initial offering of securities. It requires the filing of a registration statement. Each person who signs the statement is personally liable for its contents. The primary signatories on the statement are the officers and directors.

One of the more well-known provisions of the 1934 Act is Rule 10b-5. It prohibits the use of **inside information**, meaning information not readily available to the public.

Inside information may not be utilized in trading shares, and it is applicable to all share transactions, not just those of publicly-traded corporations. Thus, a director or an officer who knows that the corporation is about to undertake an act, such as a merger, that will increase the value of its shares is not free to purchase shares of the corporation in anticipation of their increase in value. The proscription is also applicable to others outside the corporation who are in a position to obtain information ahead of the public – for example, employees of a law firm or an accounting firm who are working on the merger transaction.

**Protection from Liability**

The risk of personal liability as described above presents a grim picture for directors and officers. There are, however, avenues available to protect themselves from personal liability.

A statute may provide that a director is not liable even for unwise decisions that caused damage to the corporation if the act or omission was made in good faith or did not involve intentional misconduct or a knowing violation of the law.

But a director cannot be excused from liability for

- a transaction from which the director received an improper benefit, whether or not the benefit resulted from an action taken within the scope of the director's office

- an act or omission for which the liability of a director is expressly provided by statute or

- an act related to an unlawful stock repurchase or payment of a dividend.

**Indemnification**

A corporation may indemnify (pay legal expenses for) a person who was, is, or is threatened to be named as a defendant in a lawsuit because the person is or was a director or officer. The indemnification must be approved by a majority votes of the other directors, by special legal counsel or the shareholders, as set forth in the statute.

Indemnification is only available if the person

- conducted himself or herself in good faith;
- reasonably believed his or her official conduct was in the corporation's best interests;
- reasonably believed his or her conduct was not opposed to the corporation's best interests; and
- with respect to criminal proceedings only, had no reasonable cause to believe his or her conduct was unlawful.

## Important Terms

Annual meeting
Business judgment rule
Business opportunity rule
Classification
Derivative actions
Directors
Directors and officers insurance
Indemnification

Inside director
Officers
Organizational meeting
Outside director
Quorum
Securities and Exchange Acts
Special meeting

## Important Concepts

The board of directors elects officers, declares dividends, and makes policy decisions for the corporation.

Officers manage the day-to-day operations of the corporation.

Officers and directors may be held personally liable if they breach the fiduciary duties they owe to the corporation and to the shareholders.

Under certain circumstances, the corporation may indemnify directors and officers for their corporate acts.

# Chapter Fourteen

# OPERATION OF THE CORPORATION

Once the corporation has been formed, careful attention should be given to operating it and maintaining its records in an accurate, accessible manner.

## Obtaining Subchapter S Status

The designations "Subchapter C corporation" and "Subchapter S corporation" come from the Internal Revenue Code of 1986, as amended (the "Code" or the "IRC").

Pursuant to § 1361(3) of the Code, a C corporation is a regular corporation that is taxed twice, once on the income of the corporation and once on the distributions of income to the shareholders in the form of dividends. Most corporations are C corporations.

Pursuant to § 1361(a)(1) of the Code, an S corporation is taxed as if it were a partnership. The income of the corporation flows through to the shareholders and is taxed only once. In effect, the income of the corporation itself is not taxed at all; only the shareholders' income is subject to federal taxation.

Because of this significant tax advantage, only small businesses are permitted to elect Subchapter S status. For Subchapter S election purposes, pursuant to § 1361(b) of the Code, a small business

- is a domestic corporation. In this case, "domestic" means a corporation formed in one of the United States as opposed to a foreign country. (See, in contrast, a state's use of the terms "domestic" and "foreign," and "alien" in Chapter Nine.) For federal tax purposes, Subsection 1361(b)(1) of the Code defines a domestic corporation as one that is either incorporated under the laws of the United States or the laws of any state. In other words, it is not an alien corporation, incorporated under the laws of another country.

- is not subject to tax treatment under other provisions of the Code.

- has no more than 75 shareholders, but the Code treats a married couple as a single shareholder.

- has only certain persons as shareholders. No partnerships, limited liability companies, or business corporations are permitted to hold shares in an S corporation. The estate of a shareholder may remain a shareholder for a certain period after the shareholder dies. Some trusts are permitted to be Subchapter S shareholders. Nonprofit entities may hold shares.

- has no nonresident alien shareholders. Each shareholder who is a natural person must be a United States citizen or a resident alien.

- has only one class of shares. No preferred shares are permitted, only common.

The corporation's board of directors must authorize election of Subchapter S status and see that the election is actually made by filing an IRS Form 2553.

Pursuant to § 1362(a)(2) of the Code, each shareholder and each spouse who may have a community property interest in the shares must execute the Form 2553.

Pursuant to § 1362(a)(3) of the Code, if the election is to cover the first taxable year in which the business is incorporated, the election must be made no later than the fifteenth day of the third month of that year.

The best method is to obtain the signatures of shareholders and spouses and file the Form 2553 as promptly as possible. Use a method of delivery through which you can verify the date when the application was received at an IRS office.

Pursuant to § 1362(d) of the Code, Subchapter S election remains effective until terminated or revoked.

**Qualifying the Corporation in Other States**

The corporation may have to seek authority to transact business in other states. This action should not be taken carelessly, for doing so subjects the corporation to taxation in each state. If, however, the corporation is indeed carrying on business, it must qualify pursuant to the statutes and procedures outlined by the host state.

Each state promulgates its own forms and sets its own fees for a certificate of authority or amended certificate of authority. Many states have placed the necessary documents on the Internet for easy access.

A certificate from the state of domestication verifying the actual existence of the corporation must accompany the application for a certificate of authority in a foreign state. This certificate is usually available from a secretary of state.

**Maintenance of Records**

A database may be the solution for persons charged with maintaining records for numerous corporations. The primary source must be the written minute books, but the information contained therein can be entered into a database for faster retrieval. One may build a database or purchase one of the many designed for this specific recordkeeping purpose.

**Drafting Authorizing Resolutions**

Drafting resolutions of the shareholders, the board of directors, or committees of the board of directors is an accepted way of operating the corporation on a day-to-day basis.

While a menu of resolutions is beyond the scope of this book, there is a wealth of form books offering resolutions for every conceivable topic with which a corporation may deal, including extolling the qualities of a deceased board member. These may be found in most law libraries.

Brief sample resolutions are available in the appendices.

### Obtaining Certificates from Agencies

The corporation may have to prove it exists and that it is current in payment of its taxes. This proof can be obtained from state agencies.

Most secretaries of state issue a single **certificate of good standing** as evidence that a corporation is in existence in the state and that the corporation has paid all taxes levied to date.

In some states – notably California and Texas – there are two documents. In each state the secretary of state issues a **certificate of existence** that shows only one fact: existence as of the date of the certificate. To obtain a statement of taxes paid, you must go to the California Franchise Tax Board or the Texas Comptroller of Public Accounts for a **certificate of good standing**.

The certificate of good standing that specifies the corporation is eligible to be dissolved is referred to as a **certificate of status**.

Delaware offers both a long form and a short form certificate of good standing, with the fee for the latter considerably less. The short form certifies existence and, upon request, certification of payment of taxes to date. The long form lists every filing, and the effective date of that filing, that has been made concerning that corporation with the Delaware Department of Corporations.

### Creating Internal Certificates of Officers

An officer of a corporation may be required to certify personally to certain facts in a " Certificate of President" or " Certificate of Secretary" or " Certificate of Officer." In this case the officer is certifying to facts of which he or she has personal knowledge due to the office the person holds within the corporation.

Frequently an officer will certify to the accuracy of exhibits attached to his or her certificate, such as:

- the articles of incorporation and all amendments thereto as of the date of the certificate

- the bylaws of the corporation and all amendments thereto as of the date of the certificate

- resolutions adopted by the shareholders or board of directors, usually dealing with the specific transaction at hand

- the incumbency of officers and the authenticity of the signature of each officer who will be executing documents on behalf of the corporation.

## "Bringdown" Certificates

If a substantial time has elapsed between the date of a certificate and the actual date of a transaction's closing, the officer may be asked to give a further "bringdown" Certificate of No Change, stating that no changes have occurred since the date of the original certificate.

A "bringdown" certificate from a state agency means a certificate covering the time period from an original certificate to the present. You may need to "bringdown" a Uniform Commercial Code search, for example, or "bringdown" a certificate of good standing. The "bringdown" assures all parties that nothing substantial has changed since the original certificate was issued.

A "bringdown" may be obtained by e-mail, fax, telex, or verbal confirmation of a clerk in the agency.

## Managing Corporate Events

The corporation may enter into substantial transactions, such as the purchase of real estate. If successful as a private corporation, it may decide to make an **initial public offering** or IPO of its shares to the public. It may merge or convert, as discussed in Chapter Fifteen.

## Important Terms

| | |
|---|---|
| Bringdown | Corporate maintenance |
| C corporation | Form 2553 |
| Certificate of existence | Initial public offering |
| Certificate of good standing | Officer's certificate |
| Certificate of status | S corporation |

## Important Concepts

Pursuant to paragraph 1361(a)(1) of the Code, a Subchapter S corporation is taxed as if it were a partnership. The income of the corporation flows through to the shareholders and is taxed only once.

Only small businesses are permitted to elect Subchapter S status.

Each shareholder and each spouse who may have a community property interest in the shares must execute the Form 2553 filed with the IRS to elect Subchapter S status.

Most states issue a single certificate of good standing as evidence that a corporation, whether domestic or foreign, is in existence in the state and the corporation has paid all taxes due and payable to date.

Some states issue two documents: a certificate of existence and a separate certificate of good standing addressing payment of taxes.

A "bringdown" certificate certifies that facts have not changed during a specific time period beginning with the issue date of the original certificate being verified.

# Chapter Fifteen

# DISSOLUTION OF THE CORPORATION

A corporation's **dissolution** can be voluntary or involuntary. It can be triggered by specific events or be the result of special transactions, such as a corporation's sale of all or substantially all of its assets.

Just as in the partnership form of business, termination of the corporation involves the dissolution of the separate legal entity created by incorporation. Dissolution is not, however, synonymous with **liquidation**.

Dissolution involves the breaking up of the entity, while liquidation is the conversion of the entity into a " liquid" form. Although the two often go hand-in-hand, it is possible for a corporation to dissolve and then reincorporate as a new corporation with largely the same assets as the old one. A dissolving corporation may or may not liquidate its assets.

There are two types of dissolution: voluntary and involuntary.

**Voluntary Dissolution**

Voluntary dissolution can be accomplished by the incorporators, the directors, or the shareholders.

The corporation seeking to dissolve voluntarily must

- pay any taxes it owes and receive a certificate confirming the payment;
- file articles of dissolution; and
- pay the appropriate filing fee.

Articles of dissolution may only be filed when all liabilities and obligations of the corporation have been paid or provision has been made to do so. Any remaining property and assets must be distributed to shareholders according to their respective rights and interests.

Before filing articles of dissolution the corporation must also:

- cease all business except that necessary to wind up its affairs;
- notify all creditors and claimants of its intent to dissolve; and
- collect its assets, discharge its debts, and distribute its assets.

Articles of dissolution filed for an operating corporation generally must state that

- all debts have been taken care of and that all assets have been applied for payment thereof and no property remains; or
- there are no pending suits or that provision has been made for payment of any judgment that might result.

## Corporations That Have Issued Shares

If the corporation has shareholders, it must obtain their consent to dissolve, either by an affirmative vote at a properly noticed meeting or a written consent given in lieu of such meeting. The secretary of state will want to know the number of shares outstanding and number of shares that voted in favor of dissolution. Each outstanding share of the corporation is entitled to vote on a dissolution resolution, regardless of voting restrictions on the shares pursuant to the articles of incorporation.

Shareholders who dissent have the right, under certain circumstances, to obtain fair value for their shares.

## Corporations That Have Not Issued Shares

Incorporators or directors can voluntarily dissolve a corporation only if the corporation has not yet commenced business or issued shares.

The articles of dissolution must be executed by a majority of the incorporators or directors and must state that the corporation has not commenced business, has not issued any shares, has no unpaid debts, and has returned any amounts paid for share subscriptions.

## Ceasing to Exist

Upon completion of proper procedures under the controlling statute, a secretary of state will issue a **certificate of dissolution**. Upon receipt of the certificate of dissolution, the corporation ceases to exist.

A dissolved corporation is usually allowed a certain number of years to wind up its affairs and bring any legal actions concerning corporate activities.

## Revocation of Voluntary Dissolution

Within a time period specified by the enabling statute, the voluntary dissolution proceedings can be revoked by a resolution of the parties that originally consented to the dissolution. The notice of revocation must be duly filed everywhere the original articles of dissolution and any related surrendering of certificates of authority were filed.

## Nonvoluntary Dissolution

Various state bodies, such as the courts, the secretary of state, and the attorney general, have power to dissolve a corporation involuntarily.

## Action by a Court

The court can dissolve a corporation when it finds that the corporation has committed one or more of the following acts of default:

- failed to comply with a condition precedent to incorporation;
- procured original articles or any amendments through fraud;
- transacted business beyond scope of purpose; or
- misrepresented material facts in any document submitted by the corporation.

*Action by a Secretary of State*

A secretary of state can dissolve a corporation if the corporation has

- failed to file a required report or pay fees in a timely manner; or
- failed to maintain a registered agent; or
- paid a filing fee for the articles or initial franchise tax with a dishonored check.

Before it can dissolve the corporation, a secretary of state must provide the corporation with notice of its violations, which gives the corporation an opportunity to cure the default. If the default is not remedied, the secretary of state will issue a certificate of dissolution, and the corporation will cease to exist.

Any corporation administratively dissolved by the secretary of state, however, can (within a certain time period) pay a fee and file an application for reinstatement. If the corporation establishes to the satisfaction of the secretary of state that the default has been cured or that there was no cause for the dissolution, the secretary of state will reinstate the corporation and issue a certificate of reinstatement. If the reinstatement is retroactive, the corporation will be deemed to have existed without interruption.

*Action by an Attorney General*

An attorney general can dissolve a corporation involuntarily if the corporation has been convicted of a felony or if a high-ranking managerial agent of the corporation is convicted of a felony in the conduct of the affairs of the corporation.

Any dissolution by an attorney general must be deemed to be in the public interest and must involve a persistent course of felonious conduct on the part of the corporation or high-ranking managerial agent. Unlike the involuntary dissolution procedures initiated by the secretary of state, there is no notice and opportunity to cure.

## Important Terms

Application for reinstatement          Dissolution
Articles of dissolution               Involuntary dissolution
Certificate of reinstatement          Liquidation
Certificate of dissolution            Voluntary dissolution

## Important Concepts

The business performed by the corporation can be dissolved by
voluntary dissolution or involuntary dissolution.

Shareholders who dissent have the right, under certain circumstances, to
obtain fair value for their shares.

# Chapter Sixteen

# THE LIMITED
# LIABILITY COMPANY

## Background

In 1977 Wyoming became the first state to authorize the creation and operation of a **limited liability company** or "**LLC**." Wyoming was followed in 1982 by Florida, which created the entity to entice foreign investment into the state. In 1990 Colorado became the third state to adopt LLC legislation, with Utah, Virginia, Kansas, Nevada and subsequently Texas.

Each state now provides for forming and operating an LLC. The National Conference of Commissioners of Uniform State Laws is drafting a uniform LLC Act, and the American Bar Association's Partnership and Unincorporated Business Organizations Committee has provided information to utilize in drafting an LLC statute.

This nationwide acceptance of the LLC form of doing business has removed one of the two doubts that originally held people back from using the form. What if one wished to qualify to do business in a state that did not provide for LLCs? This possibility no longer exists.

The second doubt – the attitude of the Internal Revenue Service concerning whether the entity would be taxed as a partnership or a corporation – was removed by the 1997 amendment to the federal tax code allowing the taxpayer to check whether it wishes to be taxed as a partnership or as a corporation.

States provided for the creation of the LLC as a result of various pressures from private and business communities, including:

- providing innovative methods for transacting business in the state, thereby enticing new businesses that generate more income for the state;

- protecting personal assets of participants from creditors of the business venture; and

- avoiding taxation as much as possible without significant formalities or restrictions.

The LLC offers its members an attractive combination of limited liability and favorable federal tax treatment. In other words, it combines the primary advantages of the business corporation and the partnership.

An LLC possesses *both* the limited liability found in the corporate form *and* the favorable federal tax treatment of the partnership form. The participants in the LLC are thus offered insulation from personal liability while enjoying full pass-through status for federal tax purposes.

In addition, the LLC permits hands-on management by its members – a great advantage to some business persons who do not wish to delegate authority and decision-making.

The LCC is thus considered by many businesspersons to combine the best of both worlds: limited liability, favorable tax treatment, and management by members. It is not limited in its number of owners, as is the Subchapter S corporation, nor in who those owners may be. An LLC seeking to raise capital may lawfully offer membership to corporations, partnerships, or other LLCs.

The LCC has its own vocabulary. As a point of reference, compare key terms of the business corporation to those of the LLC:

| Business Corporation | LLC |
|---|---|
| Owners/Shareholders | Members |
| Directors | Managers |
| Officers | Officers |
| Incorporator | Organizer |
| Articles of Incorporation | Articles of Organization |

| Business Corporation | LLC |
| --- | --- |
| Bylaws | Operating Agreement<br>Or<br>Regulations |

or, with the limited partnership:

| Limited Partnership | LLC |
| --- | --- |
| Partners | Members |
| General Partner(s) | Manager(s) |
| Certificate of Limited Partnership | Articles of Organization |
| Partnership Agreement | Operating Agreement<br>or<br>Regulations |

*Domestic and Foreign LLCs*

Like corporations and limited partnerships, LLCs are categorized as domestic and foreign. Name availability, therefore, should include a check of other states in which the LLC expects to qualify to do business. The final decision on whether or not the name is available is made when the articles of organization or application to qualify to do business are submitted to the state officials for filing.

*Members*

A **member** in the LLC is synonymous with an owner/shareholder in the corporate form of doing business or with a partner in the partnership form of doing business. Any person can be a member of an LLC. "Person," as defined by the enabling statute, generally includes the following:

- a natural person with legal capacity
- a general partnership
- a limited partnership

- another LLC, either domestic and foreign
- a trust or the trustee thereof
- an estate or the executor or administrator thereof
- a corporation, either for profit or nonprofit and
- a custodian, a nominee, or any entity in a representative capacity.

Members may be divided into classes or groups with certain express duties, powers, and rights, including voting rights.

## Managers and Officers

Except to the extent that the articles of organization or the operating agreement reserve management of the LLC to the members, the business affairs of the LLC are managed under the direction of a **manager** or managers.

Managers manage the LLC similarly to the way directors manage the corporation. Managers are not required to be residents of the state in which the LLC was formed or to be a member of the LLC.

Managers may also designate **officers** to perform certain delegated functions, calling them by the titles the public is accustomed to hearing, such as "president" or "secretary."

## Organizer

Like the incorporator of a corporation, the **organizer** of the LLC is the person who files the articles of organization creating the LLC.

## Operating Agreement or Regulations

States give different names to the document that sets forth the rules under which the LLC will operate. Most use "**operating agreement**," while some states provide for operation by resolutions of the managers or members.

The operating agreement (or, as called in some states, **regulations**) that sets forth the LLC's policies and procedures is equivalent to the bylaws of the corporation.

In operation, the structure and application on an operating agreement is more akin to a partnership agreement than to corporate bylaws. The operating agreement may contain any provisions for the regulation and management of the affairs of the LLC that are not inconsistent with the law or the articles of organization.

**Articles of Organization**

An LLC is formed by filing **articles of organization** with the appropriate state agency. The articles of organization are similar to the articles of incorporation that are filed for corporate existence. They provide basic information regarding the LLC and its participants.

At a minimum, most states require that the articles of organization must contain the following information:

- name
- duration
- purpose
- address of the initial registered office and name of the initial registered agent at that address
- statement that the LLC is to be managed by a manager or managers or statement that it will be managed by members
- name and address of each initial manager or managers, if applicable, or each initial member
- name and address of each organizer.

The articles may contain any other provisions not inconsistent with law. If the articles meet all of the necessary statutory requirements, the state official will issue a certificate of organization that evidences commencement of the legal existence of the LLC.

## Name

Availability of the name is usually the first matter that must be determined. It is wise to determine a first choice of name and one or two alternatives. The criteria for the name of the LLC are similar to that of the limited partnership and the corporation, and a desired name may not be available for use.

Most states have established three criteria for the name of an LLC. First, the name of an LLC cannot be the same as, or deceptively similar to, the name of any domestic or foreign LLC, corporation, or limited partnership nor any reserved or registered name for such entity.

Second, the name of an LLC cannot contain any word or phrase that implies that it is organized for any purpose or purposes other than that stated in its articles of organization.

Third, the name must include a specific designation to identify that it is an LLC. Various states allow such variations as "Limited Liability Company" or "Limited Company" or the abbreviations "L.L.C.," "LLC," "L.C.," or "LC."

An LLC may transact business under an assumed name by filing an assumed name certificate as prescribed by law. LLCs may reserve the exclusive right to use a name in a state by filing an application to reserve the name with that state's secretary of state.

## Duration

The duration of the LLC may be perpetual or a time certain, depending on the enabling statute and the desires of its members.

## Purpose

A brief statement is required in the articles of organization that the LLC will transact any or all lawful business for which it may be organized. This general statement is preferred over a specific description of the purpose to prevent the LLC's being restricted from engaging in additional business in the future.

It is, however, important to note that any act by a manager, officer, or member of the LLC for the purpose of carrying on the business of the LLC binds the LLC. An apparent authority dilemma can, therefore, arise by using the phrase "any or all lawful purpose." Members should be aware of this problem and decide if more specific language should be used in the articles of organization.

## *Registered Office and Registered Agent*

Like the corporation and the limited partnership, the LLC must continuously maintain a registered agent and registered office. Failure to do so can subject the company to involuntary dissolution.

## *Election of Management*

The articles of organization must include information regarding the manner in which the LLC is to be managed. The company may either be managed by its members or by managers that are elected by the members.

## Operating Agreement

Unless otherwise provided in the articles of organization, the initial operating agreement of the LLC should be adopted by the members or managers, if any, named in the articles of organization.

Due to the flexibility in drafting, an operating agreement is more similar to a partnership agreement than to bylaws. For example, the operating agreement contains the following information that is not contained in most bylaws:

- purpose of the LLC
- method of management of the LLC
- method and manner of initial capital contributions
- allocation of profits and losses

- method and manner of transferring membership interests
- events triggering dissolution and method for continuation.

It is customary to require all of the members and managers, if any, to sign the operating agreement to indicate their acceptance and acknowledgment of the terms and conditions set forth in the agreement.

Like the bylaws and articles of incorporation of a corporation, the LLC's operating agreement and articles of organization must not conflict.

## Membership

The operating agreement may provide that a member's membership interest be evidenced by a certificate of membership interest. There are, however, generally no requirements prescribed by law regarding the format or information required on the certificate. Note, in contrast, the lengthy requirements states have for share certificates.

## Contributions

The contribution of a member may be in cash, property, services rendered, or a promissory note or other obligation to pay cash or transfer property to the LLC. A promise to pay the contribution must be set out in writing in order to be enforceable. The obligation to pay the contribution is the only exception to the rule that an LLC member has no personal liability.

Moreover, the personal liability for the contribution survives the death, disability, or change in circumstances of a member and passes to the member's legal representative or successor.

The possible consequences for failure of a member to make a contribution are

- reduction of the defaulting member's percentage or other interest in the LLC
- subordination of the member's interest to that of the nondefaulting members

- forced sale of the member's interest
- forfeiture of the member's interest
- lending of money to the defaulting member by other members of the amount necessary to meet the defaulting member's commitment
- determination of the value of the defaulting member's interest by appraisal or by formula and redemption or sale of the interest at that value
- other penalty or consequence set out in the operating agreement.

## Qualifying as a Foreign LLC

Like a foreign corporation or a foreign limited partnership, a foreign LLC must qualify before doing business in another state. An application for a certificate of authority is filed with the appropriate state official, along with the filing fee and a certificate issued by the domestic state certifying the existence of the LLC.

Upon the issuance of a certificate of authority by the state official, the foreign LLC is authorized to transact business in the foreign state. Generally, the LLC statutes' provisions for withdrawal or termination of a foreign LLC, revocation of a foreign LLC's certificate of authority, and consequences of a foreign LLC's transacting business without authority are similar to the provisions of the corporation acts.

## Operation in the Normal Course of Business

The LLC must maintain records of its operation. Generally, it is required to maintain the following information:

- a list containing the name, address, and percentage of ownership of each member by class or group
- copies of federal, state, and local tax returns for the six most recent tax years
- copies of the articles of organization and operating agreement, amendments to both, powers of attorney, and any documents that create classes or groups of members
- documentation concerning contributions

- record of the date on which each member became a member and
- correct and complete accounting records/books.

## Management

*Manager/Members or Elected Managers*

One of the advantages of the LLC form of doing business is the flexibility it offers in the methods of management. LLCs may be managed by its members, like a closely held corporation. There is no governing body other than the owners/members.

Voting members of the LLC may decide to centralize their management and be governed by a body similar to the board of directors of a corporation. This group is called the **managers**. Only one manager is required to be elected.

*Officers*

The manager possesses the authority to delegate his or her management duties and designate one or more persons as **officers**. Both the officers and managers (as well as the members) are agents of the LLC. They can bind the company, unless they lack authority and the third party with whom they are dealing has knowledge of this fact.

*Limited Liability*

The greatest advantage of the LLC is the insulation it offers from personal liability. Members are not held personally liable for the debts and obligations of the LLC. Moreover, they do not forfeit this insulation, as in a limited partnership, if they participate in the operation of the company.

Members, managers, and officers may, however, be held personally liable under various environmental and federal tax laws. The LLC may provide for the indemnification of managers, officers, employees, agents and others to the same extent a corporation may so indemnify.

## Members' Rights

*Voting*

Members may be divided into classes or groups with certain relative rights, powers, and duties, with voting rights based on the member's ownership interests.

*Distributions*

Unless otherwise provided in the operating agreement, profits and losses of the LLC are allocated among the members in accordance with the ownership percentage or other interest in the LLC. Distributions of cash or other assets of the LLC are made on the basis of the agreed value of the contributions made by each member.

Interim distributions can be made before a member's withdrawal from the LLC, before the winding up of the LLC, or for any other reason stated in the operating agreement. Distributions can not be made if such distributions would render the LLC insolvent.

*Transferability of Interest*

A membership interest in the LLC is personal property and is assignable. The assignment entitles the assignee to be allocated income, gain, loss, deduction, credit, and to receive distributions. The assignee does not have any liability as a member solely as a result of the assignment. The assignee is not entitled to participate in the management and affairs of the LLC or to become, or exercise any rights of, a member. Until the assignee becomes a member, the assignor member continues to be a member and to have the power to exercise any unassigned rights or powers of a member. This process is similar to that of transferring a partnership interest.

*Voice in Admitting New Members*

After the formation of the LLC, a person can become a new member by acquiring a membership interest directly from the LLC as prescribed by the operating agreement. If the operating agreement is silent as to this process, a new member can be admitted with the written consent of all of the members.

In the case of an assignee of a membership interest, he, she, or it may become a member as prescribed by the operating agreement or with the unanimous consent of the members.

## The Professional LLC ("PLLC")

States have provided for persons who offer a professional service to utilize the LLC form by organizing a **professional limited liability company**. "Professional service" is defined in one state as "any type of personal service that requires as a condition precedent to the rendering of the service the obtaining of a license, permit, certificate of registration, or other legal authorization, including the personal service rendered by an architect, attorney-at-law, certified public accountant, dentist, doctor, physician, public accountant, surgeon, or veterinarian."

The PLLC files articles of organization that contain, in addition to the information required under the LLC Act, a statement that the LLC is a PLLC and a description of the one specific kind of professional service to be rendered by the PLLC. As with the professional corporation, only persons who are individually licensed or otherwise authorized to perform the service can be members, managers, or officers of the PLLC.

## Changes in Structure

Unless restricted by its enabling statute, an LLC may amend its articles of organization, merge with one or more entities (but not with a nonprofit entity), or convert to some other form of doing business.

## Dissolution

Generally, the LLC will continue to operate until

- the fixed period of its duration expires;
- it dissolves pursuant to its operating agreement;

- except as provided in the regulations, upon the death, expulsion, withdrawal, bankruptcy, or other event which terminates the continued membership of a member;
- the members decide to dissolve, or
- a decree of judicial dissolution is entered against the LLC.

## Important Terms

| | |
|---|---|
| Articles of organization | Operating agreement |
| Certificate of organization | Organizer |
| Managers | Professional LLC |
| Members | Regulations |

## Important Concepts

The limited liability company form combines the primary advantages of the general business corporation and the partnership: insulation from personal liability and favorable federal tax treatment.

A limited liability company is created by filing articles of organization with the appropriate state agency.

Procedures concerning name availability, maintaining a registered agent, foreign qualification, and dissolution of a limited liability company are similar to those for the general business corporation.

Persons meeting the state's requirements may form a professional limited liability company.

# Chapter Seventeen

# CHANGES IN STRUCTURE

Significant changes to a business entity can result in, or be caused by, amendment to the articles, merger or consolidations, conversion, or sale of all or substantially all of the assets.

An original filing can be amended for some substantial reason, such as a change of the name of the entity or an increase or decrease in authorized shares.

A **merger** occurs when one or more entities are absorbed into another and one of the original entities survives.

A **consolidation** results when two or more entities combine to form a wholly new entity.

A **conversion** permits an entity to change from one form of doing business to another without having to dissolve the first entity.

The **sale of all or substantially all of the assets** of an entity may completely change the business that an entity conducts.

## Amendments

A state usually permits an entity to change the information it has on file with the secretary of state in its articles of incorporation, certificate of limited partnership, or articles of organization.

These changes are not done casually, as a significant filing fee is paid each time. The following examples will deal with corporations but may be applied to limited partnerships or limited liability companies.

The most common reason for articles of amendment is to change the name of an entity as it was set forth in the first article of the original document.

A second reason for filing articles of amendment is to change the number of authorized shares. For example, the corporation may wish to

- add a new series of shares, such as preferred, where previously only common existed;

- add a class of shares, such as dividing the common stock into Class A Common and Class B Common;

- increase the number of shares of any class or series by authorizing more shares;

- decrease the number of shares of any class or series by authorizing fewer shares;

- increase the number of shares through a **stock split**, dividing each existing share (for example, after a 4:1 stock split, a shareholder would hold four shares for every one share it previously held);

- decrease the number of shares through a **reverse stock split** (for example, after a 1:4 stock split, a shareholder would hold .25 share for every one share it previously held); or

- change the par value of the shares.

Articles of amendment require, at a minimum, the vote of a majority of the holders of voting shares. Your state may require that all shareholders, even holders of nonvoting shares, are permitted to vote on certain important questions, such as the sale of all or substantially all of the entity's assets.

Most states do not require the filing of full articles of amendment to change the registered agent or registered office. A state will provide a format at a lower filing fee, often called by a generic title such as "Statement of Change of Registered Agent or Registered Office or Both."

As long as the state's statute required only the *original* directors to be listed in articles, there is no requirement to file articles of amendment each time subsequent directors are elected or removed.

Over the years, the articles may be encumbered by so many articles of amendment that confusion results. When a corporation has reached this point, it is wise to consolidate all the changes into one document called the **restated articles of incorporation**. Restated articles are a " starting over" point; they have taken in all the amendments to date and put them into a clean, restated document.

If restated articles are filed at the same time as yet another amendment, the document is called " Amended and Restated Articles of Incorporation."

**Mergers and Consolidations**

Entities – limited partnerships, corporations, and limited liability companies – may generally merge with and into each other unless one of the entities is a nonprofit corporation. Other restrictions, such as the requirements of professional corporations, also would apply.

To effect a merger or consolidation, the controlling policy-makers of each entity must, by resolution, adopt a plan. Such a plan usually states

- the names of the entities proposing to merge or consolidate
- the name of the surviving entity
- the terms and conditions of the merger or consolidation and
- the manner and basis for exchanging/converting shares or units into shares or units of the surviving entity.

The plan may also set forth any amendments to the authorizing document of the surviving entity or other provisions relating to the merger or consolidation.

Plans for both mergers and consolidations generally must be approved by the owners of all of the participating entities.

The articles of merger or consolidation should contain

- the plan of merger or consolidation
- a statement either that owner approval is not required, or, if required, information concerning the voting of ownership units and
- a statement that the plan and its performance were authorized by the surviving entity.

If the plan complies with all formalities of every state concerned, the appropriate secretary of state will issue a certificate of merger or consolidation to the surviving, new, or acquiring entity.

The merger or consolidation may be abandoned at any time prior to the filing of the articles of merger or consolidation.

**Conversion**

For reasons of taxation, expansion, liability, or sheer convenience, managers of an entity may decide it is in the best interests of the entity to operate in some other manner.

For example, a Subchapter S corporation may wish to seek investment capital for purposes of expansion. No shares of stock may be offered to a partnership, a business corporation, or a limited liability company without jeopardizing the corporation's Subchapter S status.

If, however, the Subchapter S corporation converts to an LLC, it could offer potential investors membership in the LLC. It could also create classes of membership, where the S corporation is restricted to issuing only common stock.

Before states adopted statutes permitting conversion, one had to create a second entity, transfer all the assets to that second entity, and dissolve the original entity. Conversion statutes simplify the procedure by permitting an entity to convert directly from one form of business to another.

As with amendment, merger, or consolidation, the owners must approve the conversion.

## Sale of All or Substantially All of the Assets

The sale of all or substantially all of the assets of one entity to another entity may result in a change of structure. The sale is not one that is made in the usual and regular course of its business. It is also not considered to be a merger or consolidation.

To effect the sale, the policy-makers must adopt a resolution and receive the vote of the owners for approval. The advantage of this method is that, unless provided otherwise, the purchaser does not acquire the debts and obligations of the seller.

## Rights of Dissenters

In most circumstances, owners who do not approve the proposed amendment, the merger or consolidation, the conversion, or the sale of all or substantially all the entity's assets have certain dissenting rights.

In the case of a corporation, before the vote takes place, a dissenting shareholder must notify the board in writing of his, her, or its objection to the action.

If the action is approved without the approving vote of the shareholder, the shareholder has the right to the fair value of his, her, or its shares. In effect, the shareholder is "bought out," and the shareholder's ownership interest terminated.

Procedures for determining the purchase price or fair value of the dissenting shareholder's shares are provided by statute. Often, however, there is litigation concerning what constitutes fair value.

## Important Terms

| | |
|---|---|
| Amendment | Conversion |
| Articles of amendment | Dissenting rights |
| Articles of consolidation | Fair value |
| Articles of conversion | Merger |
| Articles of merger | Sale of all or substantially all |
| Consolidation | of the assets |

## Important Concepts

The business performed by an entity can be terminated by:

- statutory merger
- plan of exchange or
- sale of all or substantially all of the assets.

An entity may convert directly from one manner of doing business to another without having to dissolve the first entity.

# Chapter Eighteen

# THE CORPORATE PARALEGAL

The term "corporate paralegal" can mean a paralegal working in the corporate law section of a law firm. It may also apply to any paralegal working inhouse for a corporation, partnership, or other business entity.

## *Standard Corporate Duties*

The corporate paralegal working directly for a general counsel should expect to form business entities, maintain their records, and expedite their transactions. He or she will be responsible for maintaining a database or other means of tracking information about the various entities owned or managed by the company.

## *Regulatory Duties*

Regulation can be encountered on the federal, state, or local level by any company that

- has certificates of authority in other states;

- deals with the federal government in any way (environmental law, bankruptcy law, employment law, etc.);

- holds any sort of licenses or owns any sort of vehicles;

- maintains any insurance on its facilities or personnel; or

- deals with any person or entity outside of the United States.

In short, it is difficult to do business without having to conform to some sort of regulation. Paralegals track due dates, requirements, and other minutiae to keep their company in compliance throughout the nation or, possibly, throughout the world.

*"Blue Sky" Duties*

The securities specialist is a valued member of any team dealing with a publicly traded corporation. The term "**blue sky**" harks back to the days before the Securities Act of 1933 prevented persons selling a "piece of the blue sky" to gullible investors.

The blue sky paralegal tracks the requirements, and exemptions to those requirements, for registration of securities in every state and territory. He or she is familiar with the federal securities laws and the securities laws of the various states, the forms that must be completed and filed if an exemption to registration cannot be found, and the time periods involved in such filings.

Federal filings with the Securities and Exchange Commission ("SEC") are made through **EDGAR,** the Electronic Data Gathering, Analysis and Retrieval system of the SEC. EDGAR may also be used to search for information. See www.sec.gov/edgarhp.htm.

*Outside Counsel Liaison*

Paralegals who specialize in litigation can find a home within a company acting as liaison between outside counsel and the company. They may also save substantial outside counsel fees by performing standard paralegal tasks inhouse rather than paying the billing rate of outside counsel's paralegals.

*Employment Law Duties*

With the explosion of sexual harassment suits and federal laws affecting employer/employee relationships, companies need attorneys and paralegals inhouse who concentrate on and specialize in employment and labor law.

*Internet Specialist*

In every company there is at least one person who has the latest tips on home pages, universal resource locators (URLs) and other ways to get information from the Internet. While it is true that many things may change between publication of this book and lightening-speed developments on the Internet, below are two sites that have been around for some time and are useful references.

- www.nass.org. National Association of Secretaries of State. Linked to every secretary of state that is online.

- www.paralegals.org/Forums/listsubscribe.html – registration page for the corporate listserv maintained by the National Federation of Paralegal Associations (NFPA). Being on a listserv with others in your specialty can be a tremendous resource.

At a minimum you should bookmark on your computer the home page of your secretary of state and the taxing authority in your state.

## Important Terms

| | |
|---|---|
| blue sky | outside counsel |
| corporate paralegal | Securities and Exchange Commission |
| EDGAR | |

## Important Concepts

The corporate paralegal working directly for a general counsel should expect to form business entities, maintain their records, and expedite their transactions.

Duties of the paralegal working inhouse for a corporation may include regulatory, blue sky, outside counsel liaison, employment law, or Internet specialist.

---

# Chapter Nineteen

**ETHICS**

---

Attorneys enjoy the security of aspirational ethical considerations (ECs) and mandatory disciplinary rules (DRs) promulgated by their state bars.

In the absence of similar state provisions for paralegals, both major national paralegal organizations have provided ethical guides. Until licensing occurs, these codes are aspirational. That does not make them less important.

The National Federation of Paralegal Associations (NFPA) offers a Model Code of Ethics and Professional Responsibility and Guidelines for Enforcement. Like model acts of statutes, the NFPA model is available for any state or local group to adopt for its association, in whole or in part. The entire document is found at www.paralegals.org/Development/model code.html.

The National Association of Legal Assistants (NALA) has adopted its Code of Ethics and Professional Responsibility, which is found in full at www.nala.org/stand.htm#NALA Code of Ethics and Professional Responsibility.

Below are specific, practical applications of these codes to the paralegal who works for a law firm in a corporate section or an inhouse paralegal. The thoughts are directed at the paralegal who is privy to business secrets and plans and whose major tasks are maintaining records and facilitating transactions. The following is in no way meant to be a complete and encompassing view of paralegal ethics: only a snapshot.

*Client Confidentiality*

- NFPA § 1.5 A paralegal shall preserve all confidential information provided by the client or acquired from other sources before, during and after the course of the professional relationship.

EC 1.5(a)     A paralegal shall be aware of and abide by all legal authority governing confidential information in the jurisdiction in which the paralegal practices.

EC-1.5(b)     A paralegal shall not use confidential information to the disadvantage of the client.

EC-1.5(c)     A paralegal shall not use confidential information to the advantage of the paralegal or of a third person.

EC-1.5(d)     A paralegal may reveal confidential information only after full disclosure and with the client's written consent; or, when required by law or court order; or, when necessary to prevent the client from committing an act that could result in death or serious bodily harm.

EC-1.5(e)     A paralegal shall keep those individuals responsible for the legal representation of a client fully informed of any confidential information the paralegal may have pertaining to that client.

EC-1.5(f)     A paralegal shall not engage in any indiscreet communications concerning clients.

•     NALA Canon 7. A legal assistant must protect the confidences of a client and must not violate any rule or statute now in effect or hereafter enacted controlling.

The concept of client confidentiality encompasses attorney-client privilege and the work product rule, both of which case law has extended to agents of the attorney such as paralegals.

The paralegal working on a hostile takeover or an initial public offering, for example, possesses information about a client's transactions, the attorney's strategies, thought processes, work product, and/or other client proprietary or privileged information.

One aspect of confidentiality with business organizations is remembering that the organization is the client. There may be only certain natural persons with whom the paralegal should deal. The fact that an individual is employed by the client does not mean that individual is entitled to all information to which you have access. You should get from the attorney specific names of persons with whom you may communicate. Your client, to whom you owe your loyalty, is the entity itself: the company. In certain situations, the natural persons who participate in the company may need to retain their own legal counsel because their best interests may not be the same as the best interests of your client, the company.

Before you attend a client meeting, determine from your supervising attorney to what extent note-taking is desirable. Notes or memos may be discoverable in future litigation.

Minutes of meetings follow a certain format. The format does not include recording every word spoken at the meeting.

Minute books or entity records must be made available for inspection, photocopied for, or released only to authorized parties. Minute books and other important books and papers of the business organization may be entrusted to you. These should be kept in a safe place and not exposed to the view of others. No books or records should be released to a third party without specific authorization from the client or the attorney for whom you are working. Detailed receipts for any such released material must be prepared and retained.

While publicly traded entities are required to reveal certain facts to the Securities and Exchange Commission, the majority of business workings are considered confidential. These include trade secrets and know-how, future business expansion or downsizing, employment expectations, and agendas for meetings of management.

You may be privy to any or all of this information. Do not disseminate communications from your client to anyone beyond your firm. Further, the fact that someone is within your firm does not mean he or she should be privy to details of the client's business. Whether the entity is publicly traded or privately held, no confidential information must be disclosed to anyone other than those with a need to know.

Because any form of communication runs an ultimate risk of disclosure, take reasonable steps. Do not discuss client matters on a cellular phone or a speaker phone. Do not mention a client's name in a restaurant, an elevator, or any public place. Do not leave written material where it can found by those not entitled to read it. Make sure you use accurate numbers on faxes.

"Deleted" e-mail *can* be retrieved. Anything put into writing may be used as evidence or in a news story. Careless use of technology can damage the interests of your employer and its clients.

If you are sent by a potential buyer to perform **due diligence** (a review of a potential seller's books and records), you may encounter hostility or apprehension from employees of the seller. In today's business climate, a business may negotiate with several buyers before a transaction is finally consummated. The employees may try to get information from you about the proposed transaction. Remember your loyalty is to your client; you are not there to offer information.

Family, friends and fellow employees may also quiz you, particularly if you work inhouse and rumors are flying about your company. Although you may know tomorrow's headlines in the business or general news section, you must not share this information with others, before or after the media writes about the client. Strict confidentiality must be maintained. Bragging or dropping hints about "deals" on which one has worked is unprofessional. Further, under SEC rules such hints could be considered illegal insider information.

## Conflicts of Interest

- NFPA § 1.6 A paralegal shall avoid conflicts of interest and shall disclose any possible conflict to the employer or client, as well as to the prospective employers or clients.

EC-1.6(a) A paralegal shall act within the bounds of the law, solely for the benefit of the client, and shall be free of compromising influences and loyalties. Neither the paralegal's personal or business interest, nor those of other clients or third persons, should compromise the paralegal's professional judgment and loyalty to the client.

EC-1.6(b) A paralegal shall avoid conflicts of interest that may arise from previous assignments, whether for a present or past employer or client.

EC-1.6(c) A paralegal shall avoid conflicts of interest that may arise from family relationships and from personal and business interests.

EC-1.6(d) In order to be able to determine whether an actual or potential conflict of interest exists, a paralegal shall create and maintain an effective recordkeeping system that identifies clients, matters, and parties with which the paralegal has worked.

EC-1.6(e) A paralegal shall reveal sufficient non-confidential information about a client or former client to reasonably ascertain if an actual or potential conflict of interest exists.

EC-1.6(f) A paralegal shall not participate in or conduct work on any matter where a conflict of interest has been identified.

> EC-1.6(g)       In matters where a conflict of
> interest has been identified and the client consents to
> continued representation, a paralegal shall comply fully
> with the implementation and maintenance of an ethical
> wall.

If you work for a firm with clients whose shares are publicly traded, learn and follow your firm's internal trading procedures. Recheck with your firm's conflicts department before making, or allowing your broker to make, any purchase of securities. Even if you are not working on the matter of a firm's publicly traded client, the safest procedure is to avoid such investments.

Under no circumstances can you make any investment based on inside information you obtained as a result of your employment. You must not furnish inside information to any other person, including your family members. You must not use, nor allow any family member or friend to use, his or her exposure to confidential material for personal profit.

This stricture is not limited to insider trading. A law firm employee, for example, should be aware of the firm's clients that are publicly traded and, to avoid appearance of impropriety, avoid personally trading in those stocks.

It is generally agreed, however, that holdings in a mutual fund need not be monitored, as the mutual fund holder does not control the sale and purchase decisions of the mutual fund manager. The mutual fund has the characteristics of a "blind trust" in that you and the other investors in the mutual fund allow the fund manager to be your agent, purchasing and selling without your explicit knowledge.

A conflict of interest could arise from a merger situation. For example, a client of your current employer is interested in buying a company. At a former job, you have encountered that company in some manner. (Keeping a list of matters on which you have worked will refresh your memory.) A conflict of interest may or may not exist, but a *potential* conflict of interest does exist and should be disclosed promptly to the attorney managing the matter.

If it is determined that a conflict of interest does exist, you should know how to construct an ethical wall to separate yourself from all activity on the matter. (See NFPA's publication on how to construct an ethical wall at www.paralegals.org.)

*Quality of Your Work Product*

- NFPA § 1.1. A paralegal shall achieve and maintain a high level of competence.

    EC-1.1(a) A paralegal shall achieve competency through education, training and work experience.

    EC-1.1(b) A paralegal shall participate in continuing education in order to keep informed of current legal, technical and general developments.

    EC 1.1(c) A paralegal shall perform all assignments promptly and efficiently.

- NALA Canon 6. A legal assistant must strive to maintain integrity and a high degree of competency through education and training with respect to professional responsibility, local rules and practice, and through continuing education in substantive areas of law to better assist the legal profession in fulfilling its duty to provide legal service.

You owe each client and your employer accuracy, promptness, and thoroughness. Often the books and records you maintain are the ones on which persons rely in making major business and legal decisions. Whether through a database, hard copies, or both, you should maintain information in ways that it can be retrieved when you are not available.

At a minimum, you should be familiar with the corporation, partnership, and limited liability company statutes in the state where you work. You should be able to locate counterpart statutes in any state where any client for whom you work does business. This is a particular challenge for paralegals working in smaller, bordering states who may have to stay current with the acts of several legislatures.

If you do blue sky tasks, you should be able to locate and analyze the securities statutes of each state and the federal government. These statutes can change minutely and must be tracked with care.

Through continuing education and networking, you should be able to determine the most cost-effective, appropriate means to get a task accomplished – performing it yourself, delegating it within the firm, or utilizing outside support such as a service company.

Overwork can create an ethical dilemma. If attorneys ask you to perform multiple tasks with little advance notice, you can reach the point where mistakes creep in and deadlines are missed. This situation is not client service. It is an ethical obligation to learn when to say no and ask for help, just as your ability to maintain and organize documents, retrieve information promptly, and safeguard information are ethical characteristics.

*Avoiding Unauthorized Practice of Law (UPL)*

- NFPA § 1.8     A paralegal shall not engage in the unauthorized practice of law.

    EC-1.8(a)     A paralegal shall comply with the applicable legal authority governing the unauthorized practice of law in the jurisdiction in which the paralegal practices.

- NALA Canon 3.     A legal assistant must not (a) engage in, encourage, or contribute to any act which could constitute the unauthorized practice of law . . . [remainder of the canon not quoted].

- NALA Canon 4.     A legal assistant must use discretion and professional judgment commensurate with knowledge and experience but must not render independent

legal judgment in place of an attorney The services of any
attorney are essential in the public interest whenever such
legal judgment is required.

The inhouse paralegal must constantly self-police against the
unauthorized practice of law. Other persons in the company will come to
you for information on which they will base their decisions. Even
though an inhouse paralegal may be pushed to give legal advice, your
advice must be limited to business information – particularly if there is
no inhouse counsel readily available to offer direct supervision.

Paralegals who work for firms also face this challenge. Clients have
found it is faster and easier to consult a paralegal when information or
guidance is needed. The paralegal can provide the information, but never
the legal advice.

*Overly Large Gifts*

• NFPA § 1.2. A paralegal shall maintain a high
level of personal and professional integrity. (Individual ECs
not quoted]

• NALA Canon 3. A legal assistant must not [sub-
parts (a) and (b) not quoted]. . . (c) engage in conduct or take
any action which would assist or involve the attorney in a
violation of professional ethics or give the appearance of
professional impropriety.

At some point – perhaps at a holiday or after a successful closing – a
client may wish to present you with a token of thanks. The gift should be
just that: a token. Any lavish or unduly large gifts may produce the
suggestion of a *quid pro quo* situation, which leads to the appearance of
impropriety. Be alert for any out-of-proportion gift and refuse it
graciously without offending the giver.

*Disclosure of Nonattorney Status*

•         NFPA § 1.7.     A paralegal's title shall be fully disclosed.

EC-1.7(a)      A paralegal's title shall clearly indicate the individual's status and shall be disclosed in all business and professional communications to avoid misunderstandings and misconceptions about the paralegal's role and responsibilities.

EC-1.7(b)      A paralegal's title shall be included if the paralegal's name appears on business cards, letterhead, brochures, directories, and advertisements.

EC-1.7(c)      A paralegal shall not use letterhead, business cards or other promotional materials to create a fraudulent impression of his/her status or ability to practice in the jurisdiction in which the paralegal practices.

EC-1.7(d)      A paralegal shall not practice under color of any record, diploma, or certificate that has been illegally or fraudulently obtained or issued or · which is misrepresentative in any way.

EC-1.7(e)      A paralegal shall not participate in the creation, issuance, or dissemination of fraudulent records, diplomas, or certificates.

•         NALA Canon 5. A legal assistant must disclose his or her status as a legal assistant at the outset of any professional relationship with a client, an attorney, a court or administrative agency or personnel thereof, or a member of the general public. A legal assistant must act prudently in determining the extent to which a client may be assisted without the presence of an attorney.

You must disclose your nonlawyer status in all communications, including electronic communication such as listservs or news groups. (Any legal professional, even an attorney licensed in one state, faces the danger of committing unauthorized practice of law for potential legal advice given in a state in which the message sender is not licensed to practice. Confidentiality issues are enormous.)

*Pro Bono*

> • NFPA § 1.4. A paralegal shall serve the public interest by contributing to the delivery of quality legal services and the improvement of the legal system.

> EC-1.4(a) A paralegal shall be sensitive to the legal needs of the public and shall promote the development and implementation of programs that address those needs.

> EC-1.4(b) A paralegal shall support *bona fide* efforts to meet the need for legal services by those unable to pay reasonable or customary fees; for example, participation in pro bono projects and volunteer work.

> EC-1.4(c) A paralegal shall support efforts to improve the legal system and access thereto and shall assist in making changes.

Nonprofit organizations that can utilize your expertise to maintain books and records, prepare forms, and perform other tasks that do not extend into unauthorized practice of law.

Until state laws change, be wary of doing paralegal volunteer work without attorney supervision, as the nonprofit organization may turn to you for legal advice. While guarding against giving legal advice, you can still contribute your time and expertise to organizations – particularly when the nonprofit's goals and causes are those you personally support.

If you receive proper training, pro bono work can extend beyond your standard corporate duties. For two examples, see the Spring 1999 issue of the *National Paralegal Reporter* at www.paralegals.org. Laurie Mansell and Keith Gamble, both inhouse paralegals working in Pittsburgh, Pennsylvania, found opportunities for pro bono. Mansell volunteers monthly at a county program assisting abused women and men to obtain protection-from-abuse orders. Gamble assisted with the purchase of the United Way's building in Pittsburgh.

For general information on paralegal pro bono activities, contact your local paralegal association or see pro bono information on the Internet at www.paralegals.org and www.nala.org.

*Summary*

These are only a few examples of how ethical considerations enter into the corporate paralegal's daily tasks. Many other ethical issues may arise.

You should have ready access to any state or local ethics codes for paralegals or state guides for attorneys in the utilization of paralegals. NFPA has published its nonbinding ethics opinions online at www.paralegals.org. The site www.legalethics.com is specifically designed for the ethical dilemmas raised by the ever growing use of the Internet for communication and marketing.

## Important Terms

Attorney-client privilege

Client confidentiality

Conflict of interest

Disciplinary rules (DRs)

Due diligence

Ethical considerations (ECs)

Insider trading

Pro bono

Work product rule

## Important Concepts

Ethics rules are as vital for transactional paralegals as they are for paralegals working in other specialty areas.

The business organization, not its employees, is the client. Individuals who work for the client may not necessarily be privy to confidential information.

No client information can be discussed with anyone who does not need to know that information – including one's fellow employees, family, and friends.

**Agency**. Relationship between two or more parties in which one party (the agent) agrees to act on behalf of and be subject to the control of the other (the principal).

**Agent**. One who agrees to act on behalf of and be subject to the control of another (a principal) who can be bound by the acts of the agent.

**Agent for service of process**. Person authorized to receive service of process for the corporation. Also see "registered agent" below.

**Alien corporation**. For federal tax purposes, a corporation that has been formed under authority of laws other than those of any other state or U.S. territory.

**Alter ego**. The doctrine by which a court will "pierce the corporate veil" – *i.e.*, disregard the legal fiction of the independent existence of the corporate entity – to impose personal liability upon the owner(s) of a corporation. Based upon a finding that the corporate entity has been abused to the extent that it is nothing more than the "alter ego" of the owner(s).

**Amended and Restated Articles/Certificate.** Document filed (i) to compile all previous amendments to articles/certificate of incorporation into one set of articles/certificate or (ii) to compile all previous amendments to articles/certificate of incorporation into one set of articles with further amendments incorporated in the restated articles/certificate.

**Annual meeting**. Meeting of the shareholders or the directors of a corporation. Required by statute, but statute may be satisfied with a written consent in lieu of such meeting. To be held each year at a time that may be stated in the bylaws. Contrast with "special meeting," below.

**Apparent authority.** Authority of an agent that appears to third parties to exist on account of words of actions on the part of the principal or the principal's failure to deny the existence of such authority. Also known as "ostensible authority."

**Articles/Certificate of Amendment**. Document filed to amend parts of the articles/certificate of incorporation.

**Articles/Certificate of Association.** Document filed to create an association.

**Articles/Certificate of Conversion.** Document filed to convert an entity from one form of doing business to another.

**Articles/Certificate of Correction.** Document filed to make a non-substantive change, such as correcting a typographical error.

**Articles/Certificate of Dissolution.** Document filed to dissolve, or end the existence of, a entity.

**Articles/Certificate of Incorporation.** Original or restated articles/certificate of incorporation and all amendments thereto. Document that is the application for corporate existence. Must contain various provisions as set forth in a state's statutes.

**Articles/Certificate of Merger or Exchange.** Document required to be filed with a Secretary of State in order to effect a merger or exchange of shares of stock, which document primarily contains information concerning the plan for merger or exchange and shareholder approval of the plan.

**Articles/Certificate of Organization.** Document filed to create a limited liability company.

**Articles/Certificate of Revocation**. Document requesting that the certificate of dissolution issued by a secretary of state be revoked.

**Association.** Form of unincorporated entity that can be used for the transaction of business as well as for other, nonbusiness purposes.

**Authorized shares**. Total number of shares of all classes that the corporation is authorized to issue.

**"Blank check" preferred stock.** Colloquial term for preferred stock authorized in the articles/certificate of incorporation, the rights and privileges of which may be subsequently established by action of the board of directors.

**Board of directors.** Governing body of a corporation. Natural persons appointed by the shareholders to be responsible for policy and supervision of a corporation. Directors have the power to appoint officers and agents to act for the corporation, to declare dividends, and generally to set corporate policy.

**"Bringdown."** Making the information current to the date of an event; verifying the continued existence and good standing of participants to a transaction on the exact date the transaction closes.

**Business opportunity rule**. Ethical concept requiring disclosure of possible profits by an interested director (see below).

**Business judgment rule.** Presumption that an officer or director of a corporation acts with due care in making a business decision on behalf of the corporation. Shields against personal liability, except where gross negligence or willful misconduct is demonstrated.

**Bylaws**. Rules for the orderly conduct of the corporation, ranking in precedence behind the enabling statute and articles/certificate of incorporation.

**C corporation**. Usual type of business corporation. Its profits are subject to double taxation – once as income to the corporation and again as income to the shareholders, to the extent that corporate profits are distributed to the latter in the form of dividends. Contrast with S corporation, below.

**Cancelled shares**. Issued shares restored to the status of authorized but unissued shares.

**Capitalization.** Investment in the corporation by shareholders.

**Certificate of Authority.** Certificate issued by a secretary of state to a foreign corporation, limited partnership, or limited liability company granting it authority to do business in a state.

**Certificate of Dissolution.** Certificate issued by a secretary of state upon the completion of procedures necessary under the statute to dissolve a entity.

**Certificate of Existence.** Certificate issued by a secretary of state certifying that no articles/certificate of dissolution have been filed concerning a corporation, a limited partnership, or a limited liability company.

**Certificate of Good Standing.** Certificate issued by a secretary of state or a taxing authority certifying that an entity has paid taxes assessed it through a date certain. In some jurisdictions, may be combined with certificate of existence.

**Certificate of Reinstatement.** Certificate issued by a secretary of state that reinstates the existence of a dissolved corporation, where it has been shown that dissolution was not called for or that the situation that did call for dissolution has been corrected.

**Certificate of Revocation.** Certificate issued by a secretary of state revoking a certificate of dissolution. The existence of the corporation is deemed to have continued without interruption.

**Certificate of Status.** (i) Certificate issued by a taxing authority certifying that all taxes have been paid to date, or (ii) certificate issued by a taxing authority certifying that a taxable entity has qualified with such taxing authority to be dissolved.

**Certificated shares.** Shares of stock whose ownership is evidenced by paper certificates. Distinguished from " uncertificated shares," below.

**Certified copy**. Copy of a document bearing the seal of an agency of government, such as a county clerk.

**Classification of directors**. Providing for a certain number of the directors to end their terms in a specific years, so new directors are gradually joining, and older members are gradually leaving, the board. A means of combining experience with new ideas.

**Close corporation.** Elective status available to certain qualified, privately held corporations owned by a single shareholder or closely-knit group of shareholders.

**Commingled.** Mixed funds in one account that should be kept in separate accounts. For example, funds for operation in the normal course of business are kept in a law firm's operating account. Funds held in trust or escrow for clients are kept in the law firm's trust account. These must not be commingled.

**Common stock.** Class of stock issued by a corporation. So called when a corporation is authorized to issue only one class of shares. Holders have voting rights and receive dividends after preferred shareholders, if any, have received theirs. Holders are the last to share in the corporation's property upon liquidation.

**Consideration.** Something of value. The price, motive or matter of inducement received in exchange for something else. In the context of corporate law, something of value received by a corporation in exchange for the issuance or transfer of shares of corporate stock. Depending upon the statute, consideration may consist of cash, promissory notes, services rendered, or property received.

**Consolidation.** Merger or joining of two or more non-surviving entities into a new, surviving entity, that has the assets and liabilities of the non-surviving entities.

**Constructive knowledge.** See "imputed knowledge," below.

**Constructive trust.** Trust (defined below) created by operation of law against one who has wrongfully obtained legal right to property, created in order to prevent injustice and/or misappropriation of the property.

**Conversion**. Change from one form of business entity to another pursuant to an enabling statute.

**Cooperative association**. Association organized to perform activities on a nonprofit basis for benefit of its members.

**Corporate charter**. A generic name for articles/certificate of incorporation and any amendments thereto.

**Corporation**. Statutory business entity created under the laws of a state for the purposes stated in its application.

**Cumulative voting**. Means of shareholder voting whereby a shareholder may cast as many votes for director as the shareholder has shares of stock, multiplied by the number of directors to be elected. Enhances minority participation in management of the corporation. Permitted in most states and required in some states. Contrast with " straight voting," below.

**Defined term**. Word or group of words given a specific meaning, used under that meaning through the course of a document and written with initial capital letters.

**"d/b/a"** Doing business as. See " assumed business name," above, and " fictitious business name," below.

**Deceptive similarity**. Such a close similarity between a name in use and the name sought that it raises the likelihood of confusion by the public.

**Derivative action**. Action brought by a shareholder on behalf of a corporation to enforce a corporate cause of action where the corporation has failed to act.

**Director**. Member of the board of directors of a corporation.

**Directors and officers insurance**. Insurance policy designed to cover litigation expenses if a director or officer is named in a suit solely because of actions he or she took on behalf of the corporation.

**Dissolution**. In a partnership, change in the relations among the partners caused by any partner's ceasing to be associated with the carrying on of the business. In a corporation or a limited liability company, the termination of the entity's existence as a legal entity.

**Dividends**. A *pro rata* distribution of corporate earnings among the shareholders of a corporation.

**Domestic corporation**. Corporation for profit organized and chartered by a state and subject to the provisions of the state's statutes. Distinguished from a "foreign corporation," below.

**Domestic limited liability company.** Limited liability company organized by a state and subject to the provisions of the state's statutes. Distinguished from a "foreign limited liability company," below.

**Domestic limited partnership**. Limited partnership organized by a state and subject to the provisions of the state's statutes. Distinguished from a "foreign limited partnership," below.

**Double taxation**. Taxing of income at two levels – as income to a corporation and then again as income to the shareholders who receive a portion of corporate profits in the form of dividends.

**Earned surplus**. Excess of corporate assets over liabilities that is attributable to corporate profits. Contrast with "paid-in surplus," below.

**EDGAR**. Acronym for the Securities and Exchange Commission's Electronic Data Gathering, Analysis and Retrieval System.

**Emergency authority**. Type of implied authority that arises when the principal cannot be reached and immediate action by the agent is required to protect the principal's interests.

**Estate**. Assets and liabilities left by a person at his or her death.

**Estoppel**. Doctrine by which a party is prevented by his or her own acts from claiming a right to the detriment of some other party, who is entitled to rely on the first party's conduct and has acted accordingly.

**Equitable remedies**. Remedies, such as specific performance, awarded when monetary damages will not make the injured party whole. Contrast with "legal remedies," below.

**Express authority**. Type of actual authority expressly granted by a principal to an agent, either orally or in writing.

**FEIN**. Federal employer identification number issued by the Internal Revenue Service. Serves as the equivalent of social security number assigned to a natural person.

**Fictitious business name**. Name other than the statutory name of an entity. See "assumed name" or "d/b/a," above.

**Fiduciary**. One who by virtue of a special relationship of trust has certain obligations towards another, such as the duty to act in good faith.

**Foreign corporation**. Corporation for profit organized under laws of one state, which then qualifies to do business in another state. Distinguished from "domestic corporation," above.

**Foreign limited liability company**. Limited liability company organized under the laws of one state, which then qualifies to do business in another state. Distinguished from "domestic limited liability company," above.

**Foreign limited partnership**. Partnership formed under the laws of one state, which then qualifies to do business in another state. Distinguished from "domestic limited partnership," above.

**General agent**. Agent who is given tasks, usually recurring, to perform over a period of time.

**General business corporation**. Most common type of corporation. Operated for profit.

**General partner**. (i) Any partner in a general partnership or (ii) a person who has been admitted to a limited partnership as a general partner in accordance with the partnership agreement.

**General partnership**. Association of two or more persons to carry on business for profit as co-owners.

**Implied authority**. Actual authority possessed by an agent, consisting of powers incidental to those expressly given and necessary to effectuate the purposes of the express powers. Also called "incidental authority."

**Imputed knowledge**. In the context of agency law, information that a principal is deemed to possess because the agent has such knowledge, whether or not the principal actually does. Also known as "constructive knowledge."

**Incidental authority**. See "implied authority," above.

**Incorporator**. Any natural or statutory person who meets the statutory requirements to form a corporation and does form a corporation.

**Independent contractor**. Person hired by an employer to complete a specific task or project and who, generally, is subject to the employer's control only as to the end product and not as to the method of performance.

**Inherent authority**. Authority of agent that, though neither actual or apparent, can bind the principal. Created when the principal places the agent in a position to deal with unsuspecting third parties by granting the agent actual authority to perform some other act.

**Initial capitalization**. The original investments of assets by initial shareholders of a corporation at the time of incorporation.

**Inside director**. One also employed by the company, usually in an executive position such as president. Contrast with "outside director," below.

**Inside information**. Confidential information not readily available to members of the public.

**Interested director**. One who may make a profit from some action of the corporation on which he or she is entitled to vote.

**Joint and several liability**. Concept by which any general partner may bind all other general partners and the partnership. One or more parties, or all of them, are liable, and each or all may be sued by a creditor, at the creditor's option.

**Joint venture**. Entity in the nature of a general partnership, usually confined to a specific transaction or investment rather than formed for the general purpose of carrying on a business. May be organized for a specific length of time by one or more persons known as "joint venturers."

**Legal capacity**. The capacity to form a binding contract, possessed by a mentally competent natural person of adult age. Also applies to a statutory person duly organized and existing.

**Legal remedies**. Monetary remedies, such as actual damages or punitive damages, awarded an injured party. Contrast with "equitable remedies," above.

**Legend**. Language on the reverse of a share certificate setting forth any limitations on transfer of the shares represented by that certificate.

**Letter of consent**. Permission that can be obtained from a business already using a name similar to the name that a new entity wishes to use. Enables the new entity to use a name that might otherwise be deemed unavailable.

**Limited liability**. Exposure to the loss of only one's investment in a business, not the risk of one's personal assets. A characteristic of corporations, limited partnerships, and limited liability companies.

**Limited liability company**. Separate, artificial entity created by statute for purpose or purposes stated in its application for existence. Has characteristics of the general business corporation, such as limited liability, and the partnership, such as favorable federal tax treatment.

**Limited partner**. Person who has been admitted to a limited partnership as a limited partner and whose limited liability is predicated on person's lack of participation in the management and control of the partnership.

**Limited partnership**. Partnership formed by two or more persons and having as members one or more general partners and one or more limited partners. Its chief advantage is limited liability as to limited partners.

**Liquidation**. Realization on assets and discharge of liabilities, usually in connection with winding up.

**Manager**. Natural person elected by the members of a limited liability company, authorized to manage and operate the business and affairs of the limited liability company.

**Member**. Person who joins a nonprofit corporation or a limited liability company. Equivalent of a shareholder in a business corporation.

**Merger**. Absorption of one entity into another, with the absorbed entity ceasing to exist as a separate entity. The absorbing entity retains its own identity and acquires the assets and liabilities of the absorbed entity.

**Minute book**. The notebook in which a record is kept of the minutes of meetings of shareholders, directors, or committees, or written consents given in lieu thereof.

**Minutes**. Written record of what took place at a meeting.

**Natural person**. Human being, as distinguished from an artificial person such as a corporation.

**Net assets**. The amount by which the total assets of a business entity exceeds its total debt.

**Noncumulative dividends**. Dividends payable to shareholders of certain preferred stock that were not declared by the board of directors and therefore not paid to the shareholders. Noncumulative dividends do not accumulate for payment in future years.

**Nonprofit corporation**. A corporation no part of the income of which is distributable to its members, directors, or officers. Can be formed for specific purposes set forth by statute.

**Not-for-profit corporation**. See "nonprofit corporation," above.

**Officer**. Natural person chosen by the board of directors of a corporation to serve as president or secretary (or, as the board chooses, other officer) and operate the corporation in its regular course of business. Or natural person chosen by the manager of a limited liability company and delegated the manager's duty to operate and manage the limited liability company.

**Operating agreement**. In most states, the term for provisions for the management of a limited liability company. See "regulations," below. Document of the limited liability company that sets forth the terms and conditions for its operation.

**Organizational meeting**. Meeting of directors required to be held shortly after the corporation has been incorporated. Primarily for "housekeeping" purposes, including adopting bylaws, electing officers, and issuing shares of stock in the corporation. In lieu of such meeting, the initial directors may give a unanimous written consent.

**Original issue**. Shares of stock issued directly from a corporation to a shareholder, rather than transferred from another shareholder or created as a result of a stock split.

**Ostensible authority**. See "apparent authority," above.

**Outside director**. One not employed by the company but invited to be on the board of directors because of his or her business expertise. Often serves on the committee determining compensation for the executives of the corporation. Contrast with "inside director," above.

**Par value**. Value of a share of stock of a corporation as stated in its articles/certificate of incorporation. Face value. The minimum amount for which the share of stock may be sold.

**Partially cumulative dividend**. Type of preferred stock dividend that is a combination of cumulative and non-cumulative dividends.

**Partnership opportunity doctrine**. Fiduciary obligation of a partner to share with the partnership opportunities encompassed within the purpose of the partnership.

**Person**. Individual, sole proprietorship, general partnership, joint venture, limited partnership, foreign limited partnership, limited liability company, foreign limited liability company, professional limited liability company, trust, estate, corporation, custodian, trustee, executor, administrator, nominee, or entity in its own or a representative capacity.

**Personal property**. Anything subject to ownership that is not a freehold (full ownership or life estate) in real property. Includes both tangible property such as cash and intangible property, such as shares of stock.

**"Piercing the corporate veil."** A term coined by a judge to describe the process of a creditor's moving through a sham corporate entity to the assets of the corporation's shareholder. Can occur when corporate records are not kept carefully, personal and corporate assets are commingled, and regular corporate meetings are not held.

**Preemptive right**. Right of a shareholder to acquire and maintain a proportionate share of ownership by purchasing a proportionate share of additional, unissued, or treasury shares of the corporation, or securities of the corporation convertible into or carrying a right to subscribe to or acquire shares, before such shares are offered to nonshareholders. Right of first refusal. Existing shareholders "preempt" would-be shareholders.

**Preferred stock**. Class of stock when a corporation is authorized to issue more than one class of shares. Holders are entitled to preference in the payment of dividends and in the distribution of assets upon liquidation of the corporation.

**Principal**. Party on whose behalf and subject to whose control an agent fulfills the duties of agency, pursuant to an oral or written agreement between the two parties.

**Principal place of business**. Physical site from which a person conducts its business and keeps its records of due course of business.

**Private, or privately held, corporation.** Corporation whose stock is not publicly traded.

**Process.** Means by which a court acquires or exercises jurisdiction over a person or over specific property, usually meant to compel the presence of a party of the performance of some act, such as the satisfaction (payment) of a judgment.

**Professional association.** An association of persons duly licensed to practice some profession, which persons have associated themselves under the laws of a state for the purposes of performing the professional services and dividing the gains therefrom, as stated in articles of association or bylaws.

**Professional corporation.** A corporation organized for the sole and specific purpose of rendering a professional service and services ancillary to such professional service and that has as its shareholders only individuals who themselves are duly licensed or otherwise duly authorized to render the same professional service as the corporation.

**Professional limited liability company.** A limited liability company organized for the sole and specific purpose of rendering a professional service and services ancillary to such professional service and that has as its members only individuals who themselves are duly licensed or otherwise duly authorized to render the same professional service as the LLC.

**Proximate cause.** In tort litigation, legal causation that must be proved in order to recover damages.

**Proxy.** Person appointed by the shareholder of a corporation to represent that shareholder by casting the shareholder's votes on behalf of the shareholder, usually at a meeting of corporate shareholders. Also, the writing by which the appointment is made.

**Public, or publicly traded, corporation.** Corporation whose shares of stock are registered with the Securities and Exchange Commission or are publicly traded " over the counter."

**Qualify to do business**. Obtain authorization from another state for a corporation, limited partnership, or limited liability company to do business in that state.

**Quorum**. Minimum number of members, shareholders, or directors who must be present in person or by proxy before a meeting may begin.

**Ratification**. Subsequent affirmation of a voidable act. In agency law, an act originally performed without authority that the principal authorized after the fact, either by express statement or act or by failure to repudiate the unauthorized act.

**Registered agent**. Person authorized to receive service of process for the corporation.

**Registered limited liability partnership**. A status whereby a partnership files with the secretary of state an annual registration and that maintains a statutorily required amount of liability insurance, thereby limiting the personal liability of general partners for certain acts of another partner of which the first partner had no knowledge.

**Registered office**. Business address of the registered agent or agent for service of process.

*Respondeat superior*. The concept under which an employer as principal is held accountable for the acts of the employer's employee as agent while the latter is acting within the scope and course of the employee's employment (agency). Literally, " let the master answer."

**Regulations**. See " operating agreement," above.

**Reverse stock split**. Amendment to corporate articles decreasing the existing number of authorized shares by combining currently issued shares.

**Right of alienation**. Generally, the right to transfer property. The right of a shareholder to transfer (sell, give as a gift, bequeath by will) the shareholder's shares of stock in a corporation.

**Sale of all or substantially all of the assets**. Sale not made in the ordinary course of business. Essentially involves the sale of the business itself, or a part, division or department of the business, rather than a sale of goods or services of the type in which the business deals.

**Secretary of State**. In most states, the office that deals with certification and filings.

**Securities**. Instruments used as media for investment that evidence a share, participation, or other interest in property or in an enterprise, or that represent an obligation of the issuer. Shares of corporate stock are a type of security and are subject to securities laws.

**Shareholder**. The person in whose name shares issued by a corporation are registered at the relevant time in the share transfer records maintained by the corporation. In some states, a " stockholder."

**Share certificate**. Paper attesting to ownership of shares in a corporation.

**Share records or stock records**. Records containing share certificates of the corporation and stubs showing how each certificate has been issued.

**Share subscription or stock subscription**. A written commitment to purchase and pay for a specified number of shares in a corporation. May precede the actual formation of the corporation.

**Shares**. Units into which the proprietary interest in a corporation are divided, whether certificated or uncertificated.

**Sole proprietor**. Natural person initiating and operating a sole proprietorship.

**Sole proprietorship**. Business, owned and operated by a single individual, that has not incorporated and as to which there are no formal requirements or organizational expenses. It is taxed once at the individual level. Absent insurance, there is unlimited exposure to personal liability.

**Special agent**. Agent with a finite set of tasks to perform, upon the completion of which the agency is terminated.

**Special meeting**. Meeting specially called rather than regularly held. Contrast with "annual meeting," above.

**State of domesticity**. State in which a corporation has been incorporated, as opposed to one in which it has qualified to do business. The "home state."

**Stated capital**. Defined by statute, but often: at any particular time, the sum of (a) the par value of all shares of the corporation having a par value that have been issued; (b) the consideration fixed by the corporation in the manner provided by statute for all shares of the corporation without par value that have been issued, and (c) such amounts not included in (a) and (b) as have been transferred to stated capital of the corporation, whether upon the payment of a share dividend or upon adoption by the board of directors of a resolution directing that all or part of surplus be transferred to stated capital, minus all reductions from such sum as have been effected in a manner permitted by law.

**Stated value (no par) shares of stock**. Shares of stock that do not have a specific minimum dollar value for which they must be sold, but that are sold for an amount set periodically by the board of directors.

**Statute of Frauds**. Law that requires certain agreements to be in writing in order to be enforceable, for the purpose of preventing fraud and perjury in connection with the existence and terms of an agreement. Applicable to many agency contracts involving real estate as well as contracts that cannot be performed within one year.

**Statutory merger**. Merger expanding the traditional definition to include a variety of transactions, such as consolidation.

**Share certificate**. Instrument in bearer or registered form representing shares of the corporation. See "certificated shares," above, and "stock certificate," below.

**Share subscription**. Written agreement to purchase and pay for a specified number of unissued shares of a corporation on a periodic basis.

**Stock certificate**. See "share certificate," above.

**Stock power**. Language by which shares of corporate stock are assigned or transferred. Often consists of preprinted language on a share certificate or language prescribed by the corporation.

**Stock split**. Amendment to corporate articles increasing the existing number of authorized shares by dividing the currently issued and outstanding shares.

**Stockholder**. See "shareholder," above.

**Straight voting**. Procedure whereby each holder of a share of stock in a corporation is entitled to one vote. Contrast with "cumulative voting," above.

**Subchapter S or "Sub S" corporation**. Small business corporation that, having met certain requirements, elects to permit its income to be taxed to the shareholders of the corporation rather than to the corporation itself, as provided in Subchapter S of the Internal Revenue Code.

**Surplus**. Excess of net assets of a business entity over its stated capital.

**TEL-TIN**. Telephone taxpayer identification number issued over the phone by the IRS. See "FEIN," above.

**Tort**. Private or civil wrong or harm, other than one caused by breach of contract, for which the harmed individual, or someone acting on behalf of the harmed individual, can sue to recover damages. Examples of tortious occurrences include harm resulting from automobile accidents, medical malpractice, or defective products.

**Treasury shares**. Shares of a corporation that have been issued, have been subsequently acquired by and belong to the corporation, and have not been cancelled and restored to the status of authorized but unissued shares. Treasury shares are deemed to be issued but not outstanding shares and are not included in the total assets of a corporation for purposes of determining its net assets.

**Trust**. Property interest held by one person for the benefit of another.

**Uncertificated shares**. Shares of stock that have been duly authorized and issued but are not represented by a paper instrument. Contrast with "certificated shares," above.

**Universal Resource Locator**. The "URL" or address of a site on the Internet – the combination of letters and symbols to be entered into a computer to locate the page, as " http://www.paralegals.org."

**Voting agreement**. Arrangement, pursuant to an agreement that must be in writing and on file with the corporation, by which certain shareholders agree to vote their shares as a block.

**Voting trust**. Arrangement, pursuant to an agreement that must be in writing and on file with the corporation, by which shares of corporate stock are transferred to a person called the voting trustee (as defined below) and held in trust for the purposes of voting those shares at meetings of the shareholders.

**Voting trustee**. Person to whom shares of stock owned by others are transferred, pursuant to the creation of a voting trust (as defined above), in order to be voted together pursuant to a written agreement, which agreement must be on file with the corporation.

**Watered stock**. Shares of stock issued by a corporation for consideration that has been overvalued, with the result that the value of the shares is not fully paid. The holder of such shares of stock is liable for the difference in the amount by which the consideration was overvalued.

**Winding up**. With respect to a partnership, the liquidation of the partnership. With respect to a corporation, the process of collecting and distributing the assets of a corporation that is bankrupt or is unable or unwilling to continue in business.

---

# SAMPLE ASSUMED NAME
# CERTIFICATE FOR AN
# UNINCORPORATED ENTITY

---

This sample is not intended for specific use. Each state has different requirements regarding information that must be included in an assumed name certificate. Consult the statutes of your state.

### ASSUMED NAME CERTIFICATE
### FOR AN UNINCORPORATED BUSINESS OR PROFESSION

1.     The assumed name under which the business is or is to be conducted or rendered is [assumed name].

2.     The true name of the unincorporated business is [true name].

3.     The period during which the assumed name will be used is [number] years.

4.     The business will be conducted or rendered as a [sole proprietorship/general partnership/limited partnership/joint venture/limited liability company/other unincorporated entity].

5.     The name and address of [the/each] [sole proprietor/general partner/joint venturer/manager] are [name and address].

6.     The principal office address of the [entity] is [address of principal office].

7.     The name of each [town/township/county/parish/borough/ other] where business is being or is to be conducted under such assumed name is [specific name of each or all towns/townships/counties/parishes/boroughs/other].

By: *Signature*_____
[Name], [Title]

[Notary Block, if required]

# SAMPLE CERTIFICATE OF LIMITED PARTNERSHIP

This sample is not intended for specific use. Each state has different requirements regarding information that must be included in a certificate of limited partnership. Consult the statutes of your state before attempting to file a certificate therein.

CERTIFICATE OF LIMITED PARTNERSHIP
OF
[NAME OF LIMITED PARTNERSHIP]

Pursuant to the provisions of [statute] (the "Act"), the undersigned, desiring to form a limited partnership (the "Partnership"), does hereby certify as follows:

I.      The name of the Partnership is [name].

II.      The address of the registered office of the Partnership is [address]. The name of the registered agent of the Partnership at such registered office is [name].

III.      The address of the principal office of the Partnership where records are to be kept or made available is [address].

IV.      The name and business address of [the/each] general partner is [name(s) and address(es)].

V.      The effective date of formation of the Partnership shall be the day and year on which this Certificate of Limited Partnership is filed with the Secretary of State of [state].

GENERAL PARTNER:

*Signature of General Partner*
[Printed Name of General Partner]

or, if the general partner is not a natural person:

[NAME OF GENERAL PARTNER]
A [State] [Type of Entity]

By: _____

Name: _____
Title: _____

[Name and Title of Natural Person
Authorized to Sign Documents on
Behalf of the General Partner]

# CHECKLIST FOR INCORPORATION

Each person will develop his or her own checklist for incorporation. The following are some applicable components.

In what state is incorporation desired?

What is the first choice of name? second choice? third choice?

How quickly is incorporation desired? Seek a name reservation? Or check name availability and proceed with immediate incorporation?

If there is a rush, will the client pay for a service company? courier service? special handling by the secretary of state?

Is the client considering qualification as a foreign corporation in other states? Should name availability checks be initiated in those other states? If the name is available, should a reservation be made? Should overnight courier or regular mail be used?

How many shares will the corporation be authorized to issue? More than one class? Any series in a class? Blank check preferred stock?

What is the par value, if any, of each share?

Will there be any variance from perpetual existence and standard purpose language? If so, what?

Who will be the registered agent?

What is the address of the registered office?

Will preemptive rights be denied?

Will cumulative voting be prohibited?

Will agents be fully indemnified to the extent permitted by statute?

Will the limitation on liability of shareholders be specifically set forth?

Will the limitation on liability of directors be specifically set forth?

Will the possibility and resolution of conflict of interest among directors be addressed?

Will the unanimous consent of all voting shareholders be required to take action in writing in lieu of a meeting, or will action in writing by holders of the majority of shares entitled to vote on the question be permitted?

Will the board of directors be permitted to amend and repeal bylaws, or will that be reserved to shareholders?

Who will be the initial director or directors? What is the address of each director?

Will there be classes of directors?

Will there be a minimum number of shares required to take action or to call a meeting?

Who will be the incorporator(s)?

Will shares be issued immediately or deferred? If issued, to whom and in what amounts?

What is the consideration tendered by each shareholder?

In what month will the fiscal year end?

What offices will be filled? Who will hold these officers? Will the officers receive compensation?

Will standard bylaws be used, or is some nonstandard language needed? If so, what nonstandard language must be formulated?

Will there be a chairperson of the board of directors? If so, who?

Will a specific date be set for an annual meeting? If so, what date?

What is the minimum number of directors that will be required by the bylaws? If not one, then what number?

Should you order a minute book? preprinted share certificates? corporate seal?

Will the corporation elect Subchapter S status? If so:

> What is the Social Security number of each shareholder?

> Is any shareholder married? If so, what is the name and Social Security number of the spouse?

> Who is to prepare and file the Form 2553?

Who is to prepare and file the Form SS-4?

> What is the principal activity of the corporation?

> Will the corporation have employees? If so, how many are anticipated? Will they be nonagricultural as opposed to agricultural or household?

> On what date is it anticipated that wages will first be paid by the corporation?

> Who should be listed as contact person for the IRS?

Will the corporation be acting as a general partner for a partnership? (Watch for name conflicts.)

Is the corporation being formed as an acquisition vehicle in a merger? If so, is it to be the entity that will survive the merger?

Will there be a shareholders' agreement?

Will the shares be registered with any federal or state securities authorities?

Will there be a voting agreement or voting trust?

---

# SAMPLE ARTICLES FOR A BUSINESS CORPORATION

---

This sample is not intended for specific use. Each state has different requirements of what information must be included in its articles. Some states automatically award preemptive rights and cumulative voting rights unless they are specifically *denied*; other states deny preemptive rights and cumulative voting rights unless they are specifically *elected* in the articles. Consult the statutes of your state before attempting to file articles therein.

## ARTICLES OF INCORPORATION OF [NAME OF CORPORATION]

I, acting as the incorporator of a corporation (hereinafter called the "Corporation") under the [enabling statute] (hereinafter called the "Act"), hereby adopt for the Corporation the following articles of incorporation:

1.     *Name*. The name of the Corporation is [name].

2.     *Duration*. Its period of duration is perpetual.

3.     *Purpose*. The purpose for which the Corporation is organized is the transaction of any and all lawful business for which corporations may be incorporated under the Act.

4.     *Authorized Shares*. The aggregate number of shares that the Corporation shall have authority to issue is [number expressed in words] ([number expressed in digits)] of the par value of [par value expressed in words] dollars ($[par value expressed in digits]) each.

5.     *Minimum Capitalization*. The Corporation will not commence business until it has received for the issuance of shares consideration of the value of [state's minimum consideration, if any,

expressed in words] ($[state's minimum consideration, if any, expressed in digits)].

6. *Cumulative Voting Denied.* Each share of common stock shall have one (1) vote, and cumulative voting for the election of directors is expressly denied.

7. *Preemptive Rights Denied.* No shareholder of the Corporation or other person shall have any preemptive right to purchase or subscribe to any shares of any class or any notes, debentures, options, warrants or other securities, now or hereafter authorized.

8. *Indemnification.* The Corporation shall have the power and authority to indemnify any of its agents to the fullest extent permitted by law.

9. *Registered Agent and Registered Office.* The street address of the Corporation's initial registered office is [street address, city, state, ZIP Code], and the name of its initial registered agent at such address is [name of registered agent].

10. *Initial Director(s).* The number of directors constituting the initial board of directors is [number expressed in words] [(number expressed in digits)], and the name and address of [each/such] person who is to serve as a director until the first annual meeting of the shareholders or until such director's successor is elected and qualified are: [list].

11. *Authorization of Action by Less Than Unanimous Written Consent of Shareholders.* Any action required by the Act to be taken at any annual or special meeting of shareholders, or any action that may be taken at any annual or special meeting of shareholders, may be taken without a meeting, without prior notice, and without a vote, if a consent or consents in writing, setting forth the action so taken, shall be signed by the holder or holders of shares having not fewer than the minimum number of votes that would be necessary to take such action at a meeting at which the holders of all shares entitled to vote on the action were present and voted.

12.     *Incorporator*. The name and address of the incorporator are [name and address].

*Signature of Incorporator*
Printed Name of Incorporator

---

# SAMPLE ARTICLES FOR A NONPROFIT CORPORATION

---

This sample is not intended for specific use. Each state has different requirements regarding information that must be included in articles of incorporation of a nonprofit corporation. Consult the statutes of your state.

## ARTICLES OF INCORPORATION
## OF
## [NAME OF CORPORATION]

The undersigned natural person, acting as an incorporator of a corporation (the "Corporation") under the [statute], hereby adopts the following Articles of Incorporation for such Corporation:

### ARTICLE I.

The name of the Corporation is [name].

### ARTICLE II.

The Corporation is a nonprofit corporation.

### ARTICLE III.

The period of its duration is perpetual.

or

The period of its duration is until [specific date].

or

The period of its duration is [number in words] [(number in digits)] years from the date of filing of these articles by the [filing authority].

## ARTICLE IV

The purpose or purposes for which the Corporation is organized are [charitable, benevolent, religious, eleemosynary, patriotic, civic, missionary, educational, scientific, social, fraternal, athletic, aesthetic, agricultural, horticultural, for the conduct of a professional, commercial, industrial or trade association, for the conduct of animal husbandry].

## ARTICLE V

A director of the Corporation shall not be liable to the Corporation or its members for monetary damages for an act or omission in the director's capacity as a director, except that this article shall not authorize the elimination or limitation of the liability of a director to the extent the director is found liable for:

(1)     a breach of the director's duty of loyalty to the Corporation or its members;

(2)     an act or omission not in good faith that constitutes a breach of duty of the director to the Corporation or an act or omission that involves intentional misconduct or a knowing violation of the law;

(3)     a transaction from which the director received an improper benefit, whether or not the benefit resulted from an action taken within the scope of the director's office; or

(4)     an act or omission for which the liability of a director is expressly provided by an applicable statute.

## ARTICLE VI

The Corporation shall have the authority to and shall indemnify and advance expenses to the directors, officers, employees, agents of the Corporation or any other persons serving at the request of the Corporation in such capacities in a manner and to the maximum extent permitted by applicable state or federal law. The Corporation may purchase and maintain liability insurance or make other arrangements for such obligations to the extent permitted by the [enabling statute] and other applicable state laws.

## ARTICLE VII

The street address of the initial registered office of the Corporation is [address], and the name of its initial registered agent at such address is [name].

## ARTICLE VIII

The number of directors constituting the initial Board of Directors is [number in words] [(number in digits)], and the name and address of [the/each] person who is to serve as a director are [name and address of each director].

## ARTICLE IX

The name and address of the incorporator are [name and address].

*Signature of Incorporator*_____
[Name], Incorporator

# SAMPLE ARTICLES FOR A PROFESSIONAL CORPORATION

This sample is not intended for specific use. Each state has different requirements regarding information that must be included in articles of incorporation of a professional corporation. Consult the statutes of your state.

ARTICLES OF INCORPORATION
OF
[NAME OF CORPORATION]
A Professional Corporation

First.   The name of the corporation (the "Corporation") is [name].

Second.   The Corporation is a professional corporation formed to practice the profession of [profession], and no person may be a shareholder in the Corporation unless he or she is authorized by the State of [state] to practice the profession of [profession].

Third.   The Corporation shall have perpetual existence.

Fourth.   The purpose for which the Corporation is incorporated is the practice of [profession] and services ancillary thereto.

Fifth.   The aggregate number of shares of common stock that the Corporation shall have the authority to issue is [number expressed in words[ ([number expressed in digits]), each share having a par value of [number expressed in words] ($[number expressed in digits]) and each share having one (1) vote on matters that may be brought before the shareholders.

Sixth.    The street address of the Corporation's initial registered office is [address], and the name of its initial registered agent at such address is [name].

Seventh.    The number of directors constituting the initial board of directors is [number expressed in words] ([number expressed in digits]), and the name and address of [the/each] person who is to serve as a director until the first annual meeting of the Corporation's shareholders or until [his successor/her successor/the successor of each] is elected are [name and address of each director].

Eighth.    The name and address of the incorporator are [name], [address].

*Signature of Incorporator*
[Name], Incorporator

---

# SAMPLE WRITTEN CONSENT
# IN LIEU OF
# ORGANIZATIONAL MEETING

---

This sample is not intended for specific use.

UNANIMOUS WRITTEN CONSENT
IN LIEU OF ORGANIZATIONAL MEETING
OF THE INITIAL BOARD OF DIRECTORS OF
[NAME OF CORPORATION]
A [State] Corporation

(the "Corporation")

[Effective Date]

Pursuant to the provisions of [specific authorizing section] of the [enabling statute], the undersigned, being all of the directors named in the Articles of Incorporation of the Corporation, do hereby consent to and adopt in all respects the following resolutions, and the resolutions adopted pursuant to such consent shall have the same force and effect as if adopted by the vote of the undersigned at the organizational meeting of the Board of Directors.

1.      Acceptance of Articles of Incorporation. RESOLVED, that the Articles of Incorporation of the Corporation as filed in the Office of the Secretary of State of [State] on [date of incorporation], and as reviewed by the Board of Directors of the Corporation, are hereby accepted and approved, and the Secretary of the Corporation is directed to place the Articles of Incorporation in the corporate record book of the Corporation.

2.      Bylaws. RESOLVED, that the Bylaws for the regulation of the affairs of the Corporation, as reviewed by the Board of Directors of the Corporation, are hereby accepted and approved, and the Secretary

of the Corporation is directed to place the Bylaws in the corporate record book of the Corporation.

3. Officers. RESOLVED, that the following persons be, and they hereby are, elected to serve as officers of the Corporation in the capacities listed below until the successor of each shall be duly elected and qualified pursuant to the Bylaws of the Corporation:

President
Vice President
Secretary
Chief Financial Officer

4. Corporate Seal. RESOLVED, that the form of seal of the Corporation, an impression of which may appear in the margin of this Consent, is hereby approved and adopted as the official seal of the Corporation.

5. Share Certificates. RESOLVED, that the form of certificate attached to this Consent as Exhibit A is hereby approved and adopted as the form of certificate to evidence ownership of shares of Common Stock, $[amount] par value per share, of the Corporation.

6. Issuance of Shares. WHEREAS, [name], a sole proprietor who has been doing business as [name of sole proprietorship], which Sole Proprietorship (herein so called) has assets of the value of not less than $[value of assets], which assets are to be contributed to the Corporation in the manner described below; and

WHEREAS, [name] has contributed services of the value of not less than $[value of assets]; and

WHEREAS, [name] has tendered cash consideration of $[amount] to the Corporation;

WHEREAS, each shareholder has agreed to enter into that certain Shareholders' Agreement by and among the shareholders and the Corporation, and the spouse of each shareholder has given written consent thereto;

RESOLVED, that upon receipt of a Shareholders' Agreement executed by each of the prospective shareholders named above and the spouse, if any, of each prospective shareholder, the Corporation shall issue to and in the name of the persons listed below the number of shares of Common Stock set forth opposite the name of each person.

[List of Shareholders and Shares Issued]

RESOLVED FURTHER, that when such shares of Common Stock of the Corporation are so issued, such shares shall be duly issued, validly outstanding, fully paid and nonassessable.

7.    Bill of Sale for Assets of the Sole Proprietorship "[Name]." WHEREAS, as partial consideration for receipt of the assets of the Sole Proprietorship, the Corporation has agreed to assume any and all liabilities of the Sole Proprietorship, any and all debts currently owed by the Sole Proprietorship to any third party and any and all obligations of the Sole Proprietorship under any agreement to which the Sole Proprietorship is currently a party (collectively, the "Liabilities and Obligations"); and

WHEREAS, it has been proposed that the Corporation enter into a Bill of Sale, Assignment and Assumption Agreement with [name] (the "Bill of Sale") setting forth the terms of the transfer of the Sole Proprietorship's assets to, and the assumption of the Liabilities and Obligations by, the Corporation; and

WHEREAS, the forms of the proposed Bill of Sale have been submitted to and reviewed by the Board of Directors of the Corporation, and the Board of Directors believes that it is in the best interest of the Corporation to approve the same;

RESOLVED, that the assumption by the Corporation of the Liabilities and Obligations in accordance with the terms and provisions of the Bill of Sale is hereby approved in all respects.

RESOLVED FURTHER, that each of the terms and provisions contained in the Bill of Sale, and any and all actions contemplated thereby, are hereby approved and adopted.

RESOLVED FURTHER, that the President be, and the same hereby is, authorized, empowered and directed to execute and deliver the Bill of Sale for and on behalf of the Corporation, with such changes in the terms and provisions thereof as the President shall, in [his/her] sole discretion, deem necessary or desirable and in the best interest of the Corporation.

RESOLVED FURTHER, that the Corporation shall indemnify and hold [name] harmless for the payment or performance of any of the Liabilities and Obligations.

9.      Depository Bank. RESOLVED, that regular bank accounts in the name of the Corporation be opened from time to time in such banks as the President of the Corporation shall deem necessary or appropriate, wherein may be deposited any of the funds of the Corporation and from which withdrawals are hereby authorized in the name of the Corporation by the signatures of such individual or individuals as the President shall designate.

RESOLVED FURTHER, that the Secretary of the Corporation be, and the same hereby is, authorized to certify to such bank resolutions authorizing the opening of such bank accounts in such form as said banks may customarily require, and such resolutions shall be authorized as if set forth in full herein.

RESOLVED FURTHER, that the President of the Corporation be, and the same hereby is, authorized to borrow in the name and on behalf of the Corporation such funds in such amounts from such persons or such lending institutions as the President, in the

President's sole discretion, deems to be in the best interests of the Corporation.

10. <u>Fiscal Year</u>. RESOLVED, that the fiscal year of the Corporation shall end on [date] of each year.

11. <u>Assumed Name</u>. WHEREAS, the Board of Directors has deemed it to be in the best interests of the Corporation to conduct business from time to time in the name of "[Assumed Name]";

RESOLVED, that the President of the Corporation is hereby authorized and directed to file, or cause to be filed, an Assumed Name Certificate with the Secretary of State of [State] and with the Clerks of each of [County] and [County], and with such other agencies as the business of the Corporation shall in future dictate.

12. <u>Subchapter "S" Election</u>. WHEREAS, the share-holders have deemed it to be in the Corporation's best interest to elect to be treated as a small business corporation under Section 1362 of the Internal Revenue Code of 1986, as amended;

RESOLVED, that any officer of the Corporation be, and each hereby is, authorized, empowered and directed to file or cause to be filed Form 2553, Election by a Small Business Corporation, with the Internal Revenue Service within the time period prescribed by the Internal Revenue Code of 1986, as amended.

13. <u>Organization Costs</u>. RESOLVED, that the Treasurer of the Corporation be, and such officer hereby is, authorized to pay all charges and expenses arising out of the organization of this Corporation and to reimburse any person who has made any disbursements therefor.

14. <u>Authority</u>. RESOLVED, that the officers of the Corporation are hereby severally authorized to (a) sign, execute, certify to, verify, acknowledge, deliver, accept, file and record any and all such instruments and documents, and (b) take, or cause to be taken, any and all such action in the name and on behalf of the Corporation or otherwise

(as in any such officer's judgment shall be necessary, desirable or appropriate) in order to effect the purposes of the foregoing resolutions.

       RESOLVED FURTHER, that any actions taken prior to the actual effective date of these resolutions by a person who is now a duly-elected officer of the Corporation are hereby ratified, affirmed, and adopted in all respects and for all purposes.

       IN WITNESS WHEREOF, the undersigned do hereby execute this Unanimous Consent in multiple counterparts to be effective as of the date first above written.

 

*Signature*_____
[Name of Director]


*Signature*_____
[Name of Director]


*Signature*_____
[Name of Director]

---

## SAMPLE RESOLUTIONS

---

These samples are not intended for specific use.

UNANIMOUS WRITTEN CONSENT
IN LIEU OF SPECIAL MEETING
OF THE SHAREHOLDERS OF
[NAME OF CORPORATION]
A [State] Corporation

(the "Corporation")

[Effective Date]

Pursuant to the provisions of [specific authorizing section] of the [enabling statute], the undersigned, being all of the shareholders of the Corporation, do hereby adopt the following resolutions, and such resolutions, when adopted, shall have full force and effect as if adopted at a duly noticed meeting of the undersigned.

WHEREAS, effective [date] the resignation of [outgoing director] as a member of the Corporation's Board of Directors, a copy of which resignation is attached hereto as Exhibit A, has been received by the Corporation; and

WHEREAS, a vacancy therefore exists on the Board of Directors;

RESOLVED, that [incoming director] be, and [he/she] hereby is, elected to the Board of Directors to complete the term of [outgoing director], to serve until the next annual meeting of the shareholders or, if earlier, until [his/her] death, resignation, or removal from the Board of Directors.

IN WITNESS WHEREOF, the undersigned have executed this unanimous consent to be effective as of the date first set forth above.

*Signature*_____
[Name of Shareholder]


SHAREHOLDER THAT IS NOT A
NATURAL PERSON

By: *Signature*_____
      Name:
      Title:

WRITTEN CONSENT IN LIEU OF SPECIAL MEETING
OF THE SOLE DIRECTOR OF
[NAME OF CORPORATION]
A [State] Corporation

(the "Corporation")

[Effective Date]

Pursuant to the provisions of [specific authorizing section] of the [enabling statute], the undersigned, being the sole director of the Corporation, does hereby adopt the following resolutions, and such resolutions, when adopted, shall have full force and effect as if adopted at a duly noticed meeting of the undersigned.

WHEREAS, it is in the best interest of the Corporation to designate an accounting firm that shall serve as the Corporation's auditors;

RESOLVED, that [name of accounting firm] be, and it is, designated to serve as the Corporation's auditor for the fiscal year ended [date].

IN WITNESS WHEREOF, the undersigned has executed this consent to be effective as of the date first set forth above.

*Signature*_____
[Name of Sole Director]

---

# STATUTES AUTHORIZING ACTION
# BY WRITTEN CONSENT IN LIEU
# OF MEETING

---

Notes to chart:

\*       Uses " stockholder" rather than " shareholder."

\#      Unless expressly prohibited by articles or bylaws, holders of a majority of
        the shares entitled to vote on a question may act by written consent.

•       If authority is expressly granted in articles, holders of a majority of the
        shares entitled to vote on a question may act by written consent.

The chart reflects statutes that, unless the articles/certificate or bylaws prohibit
such unanimous written consent, authorize unanimous written consents in lieu of a
meeting of the shareholders or of the board of directors. Source for board: Model
Business Corporation Act, Section 44. Source for shareholders: Model Business
Corporation Act, Section 145.

See endnotes for states that allow the holders of a majority of the shares entitled to
vote on a question to act by written consent. Note that in some states this right is
available unless the articles or bylaws expressly prohibit it. In other states, the
right is not available unless expressly set forth in the articles.

Most states set forth statutory procedures concerning notification of the minority,
effective date of the action, and recording of the action in the records of the
corporation. Consult the specific statutes for details of each state.

Further, note that Maine, Minnesota and North Dakota each allow – under certain
circumstances – action by less than unanimous consent of the directors.

212

| STATE | AUTHORIZING STATUTE | BOARD | SHAREHOLDER |
|---|---|---|---|
| Alabama | Business Corporation Act | 10-2B-8.21 | 10-2B-7.04 |
| Alaska | Business Corporation Act | 10.06.475(b) | 10.06.423(a) |
| Arizona | General Corporation Law | 10-821 | 10-704 |
| Arkansas | Business Corporation Act | 4-27-821 | 4-27-704[1] |
| California | Corporations Code | 307(b) | 603(a)# |
| Colorado | Business Corporation Act | 7-108-202(1) | 7-107-104(1) |
| Connecticut | Business Corporation Act | 33-749[2] | 33.330● |
| Delaware* | General Corporation Law | 141(f) | 228(a)# |
| District of Columbia | Business Corporation Act | 29-399.37 | 29-399.37 |
| Florida | Business Corporation Act | 607.0821(1) | 607.0704# |
| Georgia | Business Corporation Code | 14-2-821 | 14-2-704● |
| Guam | The General Corporation Law | N/A | N/A[3] |
| Hawaii | Business Corporation Act | 415-44 | 415-145 |
| Idaho | Business Corporation Act | 30-1-821 | 30-1-704 |
| Illinois | Business Corporation Act | 5/8.45 | 5/7.10(a)# |
| Indiana | Business Corporation Law | 23-1-34-2 | 23-1-29-4 |
| Iowa | Business Corporation Act | 490.821 | 490.704#[4] |
| Kansas* | General Corporation Code | 17-6301(f) | 17-6518 |
| Kentucky | Business Corporation Act | 271B.8-210 | 271B.7-040(1)<br>271B.7-040(2)#[5] |
| Louisiana | Business Corporation Law | 12:81.C(9) | 12:76.A/12:76.B●[6] |

| STATE | AUTHORIZING STATUTE | BOARD | SHAREHOLDER |
|---|---|---|---|
| Maine | Business Corporation Act | 13A 711/712[7] | 620.2 |
| Maryland* | General Corporation Law | 2-408(c) | 2.505 |
| Massachusetts* | General Corporation Law | Ch. 156B, §59 | Ch. 156B, §43 |
| Michigan | Business Corporation Act | 450.1525 | 450.1407● |
| Minnesota | Business Corporation Act | 302A.239[8] | 302A.441 |
| Mississippi | Business Corporation Act | 79-4-8.21 | 79-4-7.04 |
| Missouri | General and Business Corporation Law | 351.340.2 | 351.273 |
| Montana | Business Corporation Act | 35-1-432 | 35-1-519 |
| Nebraska | Business Corporation Act | 21-2090 | 21-2054 |
| Nevada* | General Corporation Law | 78.315-2 | 78.320-2#[9] |
| New Hampshire | Business Corporation Act | 293-A:44 | 293-A:151 |
| New Jersey | Business Corporation Act | 14A:6-7.1(5) | 14A:5-6(2)#[10] |
| New Mexico | Business Corporation Act | 53-11-43 | 53-18-8 |
| New York | Business Corporation Law | 708(b) | 615# |
| North Carolina | Business Corporation Act | 55-8-21 | 55-7-04 |
| North Dakota | Business Corporation Act | 10-19.1-47[11] | 10-19.1-75#[12] |
| Ohio | General Corporation Law | 1701.54 | 1701.54 |
| Oklahoma | General Corporation Act | 1027.F | 1073.A# |
| Oregon | Business Corporation Act | 60.341 | 60.211 |
| Pennsylvania | Business Corporation Law | 1727(b) | 1766(a) 1766(b)● |

214

| STATE | AUTHORIZING STATUTE | BOARD | SHAREHOLDER |
|---|---|---|---|
| Puerto Rico* | General Corporation Law | N/A | T.14 §1715 |
| Rhode Island | Business Corporation Act | 7-1.1-39.1 | 7-1.1-30.3(a)<br>7-1.1-30.3(b)• |
| South Carolina | Business Corporation Act | 33-8-210 | 33-7-104(a) |
| South Dakota | Business Corporation Act | 47-5-11 | 47-4-4 |
| Tennessee | Business Corporation Act | 48-18-202 | 48-17-104 |
| Texas | Business Corporation Law | 9.10.B | 9.10.A• |
| Utah | Revised Business Corporation Act | 16-10a-821(1) | 16-10a-704(1)# |
| Vermont | Business Corporation Act | T11A § 8.21 | T11A § 7.04(a)<br>T11A § 7.04(b)• |
| Virgin Islands* | General Corporation Law | T. 13 § 67b | T 13 § 196 |
| Virginia | Stock Corporation Act | 13.1-685 | 13.1-657 |
| Washington | Business Corporation Act | 23B.08.210 | 23B.07.040• |
| West Virginia | Corporation Act | 31-1-73(b) | 31-1-73(a) |
| Wisconsin | Business Corporation Law | 180.0821 | 180.0704(a)<br>180.0704(b)• |
| Wyoming | Business Corporation Act | 17-16-821 | 17-16-704(a) |

Endnotes:

1.      Pursuant to ABCA 4-27-704: "Actions or proposals to increase the capital stock or bond indebtedness of a corporation may be taken without a meeting of shareholders if one (1) or more written consents, setting forth the action so taken, shall be signed by all of the shareholders of the corporation." Any other actions may be taken by written action of the holders of the majority of shares entitled to vote on the question.

2.      The Connecticut act gives two exceptions: "…directors may not by elected by action of the shareholders without a meeting of shareholders other than by unanimous written consent, or pursuant to a plan of merger." Connecticut also requires that other, nonvoting shareholders must be notified not fewer than 20 nor more than 50 days before the effective date of a consent by voting shareholders. If one-tenth of the nonvoting shareholders protest not fewer than five days before the effective date, such action may not be taken without a meeting.

3.      But note: the newer Guam limited liability company act does provide for unanimous written consent in its § 15114(E)(i).

4.      Unless otherwise provided in the articles or bylaws, Iowa allows action by written consent of holders of 90% of the shares eligible to vote on the question.

5.      Unless prohibited by the articles or bylaws, Kentucky allows, as well as unanimous action by shareholders in subsection (1), action by the holders of 80% of the shares entitled to vote on a question, as set forth in a separate subsection (2).

6.      Pursuant to LBCL Subsection 12:76.B, "If the articles provide that such a [written] consent may be signed by fewer than all of the shareholders having voting power on any question, the consent need be signed only by the shareholders holding that proportion of the total voting power on the question which is required by the articles or by law, whichever requirement is higher."

7.      The Maine statute provides, under certain circumstances, for "informal or irregular action by directions."

8.      Pursuant to the second sentence of Minnesota statute 302.A.239.1, "If articles so provide, any action, other than an action requiring shareholder approval, may be taken by written action signed by the number of directors that would be required to take the same action at a meeting of the board at which all directors were present."

9.      Unless the articles or bylaws expressly so prohibit, Nevada allows action by a "majority of voting power," except, per § 78.320.2, that if a different proportion of voting power is required for such action at a meeting, then that proportion of written consents is required.

10.     New Jersey specifies a longer list of procedures concerning notification of the minority and recording in the minute book than any other state.

11.     Pursuant to the North Dakota statute footnoted, a written consent in lieu of meeting is valid if signed by the number of directors that would be required to take the same action at a meeting of the board at which all directors were present.

12.     Per subsection (1) of the footnoted North Dakota statute, "if articles so provide, any action may be taken by written action signed by the shareholders who own voting power equal to the voting power that would be required to take the same action at a meeting of the shareholders at which all shareholders were present."

# SAMPLE OFFICER'S CERTIFICATE

This sample is not intended for specific use.

## CERTIFICATE OF SECRETARY

As required by Section [number] of that certain [name of agreement underlying a transaction], I, [name], do hereby certify that I am the duly elected and acting Secretary of [name of corporation], a [State] corporation (the "Company"), and that as such I have access to and knowledge of the books and records of the Company. I am authorized to execute and deliver this Certificate; and I further certify as follows:

1.      Articles of Incorporation. Attached hereto as Exhibit A is a true and correct copy of the Articles of Incorporation and any amendments thereto (the "Articles") as certified to by the Secretary of State of [State] on [date]. I further certify that such Articles have not been amended as of the date of this Certificate.

2.      Bylaws. Attached hereto as Exhibit B is a true and correct copy of the Bylaws of the Company effective as of [date]. I further certify that such Bylaws have not been amended or repealed as of the date of this Certificate.

3.      Resolutions.    Attached hereto as Exhibit C is a true and correct copy of Resolutions (hereinafter so called) that have been duly adopted by the unanimous written consent of members of the Board of Directors of the Company authorizing the Company to enter into the [transaction]. I further certify that such Resolutions are in full force as a commitment of the Company and have not been repealed as of the date of this Certificate.

4.      Incumbency.    The following named persons are duly elected or appointed, qualified, and serving officers of the Company

holding, as of the date thereof, and at all times since [date], the office(s) set forth below, and the signature set out opposite the name of each officer is the genuine signature of such person.

Name                    Office(s)                    Signature

_____        _____

_____        _____

_____        _____

IN WITNESS WHEREOF, I have hereunto set my hand and caused this certificate to be executed effective as of the \_\_\_ day of [month and year].

_____
[Name], Secretary

[Notary Seal, if required]

or, attestation of another officer:

I, [name], hereby certify that I am now the duly elected, qualified and acting President of the Company, that the person executing and delivering the foregoing Certificate is the duly elected, qualified and acting Secretary of the Company as indicated in such Certificate, that the signature set forth above beside such person's name is such person's correct signature, and that the certifications set forth above are true and correct as of the date hereof.

_____
[Name], President

---

# SAMPLE MINUTES OF A
# TELEPHONIC MEETING

---

This sample is not intended for specific use.


MINUTES OF A TELEPHONIC MEETING
OF THE BOARD OF DIRECTORS
OF [NAME OF CORPORATION]
A [State] Corporation


Date of Meeting


A meeting of the board of directors of [Name], a [State] corporation (the "Corporation"), was held by telephone on [day of week], [date], at [hour meeting began, including the time zone].

Notice of the meeting had been given to each member of the board of directors in accordance with the bylaws of the Corporation, or waiver of such notice had been received from each director.

Present at [street address where most of the directors were in person – probably the principal place of business] were [names of the directors gathered in person]. Present by telephone were [names of directors participating by telephone]. Each of the participants at the meeting acknowledged that each could hear each of the other participants.

[Name of chair] acted as chair of the meeting and announced that a quorum was present. [Name of secretary of the meeting] recorded the minutes.

The first topic of business was [name of first topic]. After full discussion, upon motion duly made and seconded, the following resolution was [adopted by a vote of/unanimously adopted]:

RESOLVED, [text of resolution].

The next topic of business was [name of second topic].

RESOLVED, [text of resolution].

*[Use format above through all topics.]*

There being no further business to come before the meeting, upon motion duly made, seconded, and adopted, the meeting was adjourned at [hour meeting ended, including the time zone].

_____
[Name], Secretary of the Meeting


_____
[Name], Chair of the Meeting

# SAMPLE SHAREHOLDERS' AGREEMENT

This redacted sample is used with the permission of its drafter, who cautions that it is not intended as legal advice and should not be construed as such. It is a study sample only and is not intended for specific use. Consult your attorney to draft a shareholders' agreement designed for your personal situation.

## SHAREHOLDERS' AGREEMENT

This Shareholders' Agreement (hereafter, the "Agreement") is made effective [date] by and among [name of corporation], a [state] corporation (the "Corporation"), [name] ("Majority Shareholder") and [name] ("Minority Shareholder") (each a "Shareholder" and, collectively, the "Shareholders"). The Minority Shareholder and any future Shareholder will be collectively known as the "Minority Shareholders."

### *RECITALS*

A.     The Corporation is duly incorporated under the laws of the State of [state]. It is authorized by its Articles of Incorporation to issue one thousand (1,000) Shares (hereafter so called) of common stock, par value $0.01 per share (the "Common Stock").

B.     The Shareholders own one thousand (1,000) shares of the issued and outstanding Shares, which Shares constitute all of the presently issued and outstanding Common Stock of the Corporation. The Shares are owned in the amounts shown below:

| | |
|---|---|
| Majority Shareholder | 900 shares |
| Minority Shareholder | 100 shares |

C.      The Shareholders are employees of the Corporation and have devoted their efforts and skill to the growth, development and success of the Corporation.

D.      The Shareholders agree that the success of the Corporation requires the active interest, support and personal attention of its Shareholders and, for that reason, it is not advisable to permit its Shares to go upon the open market for sale.

E.      To promote their mutual interests, the Shareholders and the Corporation desire to impose restrictions on the transfer or other disposition of the Shares of the Corporation's Common Stock.

F.      The Shareholders desire to define their rights and obligations with respect to the sale, transfer or other disposition of all of the Corporation's Common Stock now owned or hereafter acquired by any Shareholder, whether by or as a result of a merger, conversion, reclassification, recapitalization, share dividend, share split, gift, purchase, subscription or other event, including shares of any class substituted or exchanged for the Shares.

G.      The Shareholders and the Corporation further desire to anticipate and provide for the disposition of Shares should any of the parties or a future Minority Shareholder experience death, dissolution of marriage, disability resulting in termination of employment, involuntary termination of employment with or without cause, or bankruptcy.

NOW, THEREFORE, in consideration of the mutual promises contained herein and other good and valuable consideration, the receipt and sufficiency of which are hereby acknowledged, the parties to this Agreement agree as follows.

1.      **Restrictions on Transfer**. Each Shareholder agrees that the Shares shall be subject to the options, restrictions, terms and conditions set forth herein and that, except as hereinafter set forth, the Shares shall not be sold, assigned, pledged, or transferred. Any purported transfer in violation of this Agreement shall be void and shall not operate to transfer any right, title or interest in or to any of the

Shares to the purported transferee. No Shareholder may transfer the Shares in any manner that would result in a loss of the Corporation's election to be taxed as an S Corporation pursuant to the Internal Revenue Code of 1986, as amended (the "Code"), and regulations promulgated thereunder or any comparable favorable tax treatment. Additionally, the Corporation shall not issue any further Shares without the written consent of each Shareholder.

2.     **Offer to Sell**. In the event that a Shareholder (the "Offering Shareholder") desires to sell all, or any portion, of such Offering Shareholder's Shares, but does not possess a bona fide written offer from another to purchase such Shares, the Offering Shareholder shall give written notice to the Corporation of such Offering Shareholder's desire to sell Shares, setting forth the price, terms and conditions proposed for the sale. Such written notice shall constitute an Offer (hereinafter so called). The written notice shall be sent by certified or registered mail, return receipt requested, to the Corporation at its principal place of business and to each of the other Shareholders at the Shareholder's address set forth herein or any future address that a Shareholder shall designate in writing. The Shares shall then be offered to the Corporation, and then to the other Shareholders, in the same manner as applicable to offers by a Selling Shareholder (as hereinafter defined) pursuant to Section 3 of this Agreement. Any offers Shares not purchased by either the Corporation or the other Shareholders shall continue to be held by the Offering Shareholder, subject to the terms of this Agreement, and the Offer shall be deemed null and void.

3.     **Rights of First Refusal**. Upon the receipt by a Shareholder of a bona fide written offer to purchase all, or any portion thereof, of such Shareholder's Shares, the Shareholder (the "Selling Shareholder") shall give written notice (the "Sale Notice") of such Offer to the Corporation, setting forth in the Sale Notice the name and address of the proposed purchaser and the price, terms and conditions for the sale of such Shares. The procedures of this Section 3 shall apply to proposed transfers to persons who are then Shareholders and to third parties. The Sale Notice must be accompanied by a legal opinion satisfactory to the Corporation to the effect that the proposed transfer complies with applicable securities laws and that such transfer will not

disqualify the Corporation from treatment as an S Corporation pursuant to the Code and regulations promulgated thereunder. Upon receipt of the Sale Notice and opinion letter, the Corporation shall forthwith deliver a copy of these documents to the other Shareholders. The date of the Sale Notice shall be the " Sale Notice Date."

(a)     *Corporation's Option.* (i) The Corporation shall have the first option to purchase all or any portion of the Offered Shares (as hereinafter defined) upon the terms and conditions of the Sale Notice. Within ten (10) days of the Sale Notice Date, the Corporation shall give written notice to the Selling Shareholder of the number of Offered Shares, if any, the Corporation elects to purchase.

(ii) In the event any Shareholder's employment with the Corporation is for any reason terminated, whether by disability, illness, retirement, or other voluntary or involuntary termination, the Corporation shall have the option to purchase all or any part of the Shares owned (hereinafter, the " Offered Shares" ) by the Terminating Shareholder (hereinafter so called), which option the Corporation may exercise in writing to the Terminating Shareholder or the Terminating Shareholder's personal representative within thirty (30) days of the date of the Terminating Shareholder's termination; provided, however, that within forty-five (45) days following the date of the Terminating Shareholder's termination, the Terminating Shareholder's personal representative may make demand upon the Corporation to purchase all or any part of the Terminating Shareholder's Offered Shares, and the Corporation shall be obliged the purchase such Offered Shares at the price determined under Section 6 of this Agreement.

(b)     *Majority Shareholder's Option.* After the Corporation's exercise or failure to exercise its option, any Offered Shares remaining shall be offered to the Majority Shareholder for purchase upon the terms and conditions of the Sale Notice. Within twenty (20) days of the Sale Notice Date, the Majority Shareholder shall give written notice to the

Corporation and to each Minority Shareholder of the number of Offered Shares, if any, that the Majority Shareholder intends to purchase.

(c)     *Minority Shareholder Option.* After the Corporation's and the Majority Shareholder's exercise or failure to exercise their options, any Offered Shares remaining (hereinafter, the "Declined Shares") shall be offered to the Minority Shareholders for purchase on a *pro rata* basis upon the terms and conditions of the Sale Notice. Within thirty (30) days of the Sale Notice Date, each Minority Shareholder shall give written notice to the Corporation and the other Shareholders of the number of the Declined Shares, if any, that such Minority Shareholder elects to purchase. To the extent that any Minority Shareholder fails to elect all of the Minority Shareholder's *pro rata* share of the Declined Shares, the remaining Minority Shareholders, on a *pro rata* basis, may elect to purchase the Declined Shares that the other Minority Shareholders did not elect to purchase. In such event, within thirty (30) days of the Sale Notice Date, the other Minority Shareholders shall given written notice to the Corporation and the other Shareholders of the number of Declined Shares, if any, such Minority Shareholder intends to purchase.

(d)     *Branch Office Option.* Notwithstanding the above, if the Majority Shareholder is the Selling Shareholder and the prospective purchaser is an individual who intends to open a branch office of the Corporation in a location other than [city, state], the Majority Shareholder may sell a portion of the Majority Shareholder's Shares without first making an Offer to the Corporation or to any Minority Shareholder.

If any Offered Shares remain after the exercise of the options pursuant to subsections (a), (b) and (c) above, the Selling Shareholder may, for a period of sixty (60) days after the expiration of the initial thirty-day (30-day) period provided in this Section 3, sell all, but not less than all, of the remaining Offered Shares to the purchaser named in the Sale Notice, provided that (i) such Shares are sold at the price and on the terms and conditions set forth in the Sale Notice and (ii) the purchaser executes such documents as may reasonably be required by the Corporation to evidence the purchaser's agreement that first, the purchaser shall be bound by the terms of this Agreement in the same manner and to the same extent as the Selling Shareholder had previously been and second, the Shares purchased by the purchaser shall remain subject to this Agreement. If such sale is not consummated within such sixty-day (60-day) period, any further transfer or purported transfer of the Shares shall be subject to this Agreement.

4.    **Personal Liability**. In the event a Shareholder transfers all of his or her Shares as hereinabove provided, then, at the time of transfer of the Shares, the Corporation shall reasonably endeavor to secure the release of the departing Shareholder from any personal liability of the departing Shareholder on any debt or obligation of the Corporation; provided, however, that the failure of the Corporation to do so shall not give rise to any liability on the part of the Corporation.

5.    **Transfer on Death**. In the event of the death of a Shareholder (hereinafter, a "Deceased Shareholder"), within one (1) year from the date of the Deceased Shareholder's death, the personal representative of the Deceased Shareholder may, at such personal representative's option, notify the Corporation of the personal representative's intent to sell the Deceased Shareholder's Shares to the Corporation. In such case, within ninety (90) days of the receipt of such notice, the Corporation shall purchase Shares owned by the Deceased Shareholder, said notice constituting an Offer. The Shares shall be purchased for cash, and the price shall be as agreed between the Corporation and the Deceased Shareholder's personal representative. If no agreement as to value can be reached, the value of the Shares shall be determined as follows:

The Corporation and the Deceased Shareholder's personal representative shall each appoint as an Agent (hereinafter so called) a person knowledgeable by education, training and experience in the valuation of companies in the [type of business or industry] industry, and the Agents shall decide upon the Fair Market Value (as hereinafter defined) of the Shares to be purchased by the Corporation. The "Fair

Market Value" shall be that cash value that would be agreed upon by a willing and able purchaser and a willing and able seller, neither being under any compulsion to purchase or to sell, if the Shares were exposed to the market for a reasonable period of time. In the event the Agents are unable to agree upon a Fair Market Value, then they shall appoint a mutually agreeable, independent Third Party (hereinafter so called) who shall also be a person knowledgeable by education, training and experience in the value of companies in the [type of business or industry] industry, to determined the Fair Market Value, and such determination by such third party shall be binding upon all parties hereto.

For the purpose of the Agents' or Third Party's determining the Fair Market Value, the Corporation hereby agrees to grant to any Agent or Third Party ready access to any and all records of the Corporation reasonably required for the purpose of determining the Fair Market Value. Each party shall beat the cost of his, her or its Agent. In the event a Third Party is appointed by such Agents, the expenses of the Third Party shall be shared equally by the Corporation and the Estate of the Deceased Shareholder.

6.    **Involuntary Transfers.** In the event of an Involuntary Transfer (as hereinafter defined) of any Shares, the Corporation and the Shareholders shall have an option to purchase such Shares in the same manner applicable to Offers by a Selling Shareholder pursuant to Section 3 of this Agreement at a price equal to the net book value of the Shares as determined in accordance with generally accepted accounting principles (hereinafter, "GAAP") by the certified public accountants regularly retained to compile the books and records of the Corporation. Within five (5) days of the Corporation's receipt of actual notice of an Involuntary Transfer, the Corporation shall notify the Shareholders of the occurrence of such Involuntary Transfer. An Involuntary Transfer shall include:

i.    A Shareholder's making any general assignment for the benefit of such Shareholder's creditors;

ii.     A Shareholder's filing a voluntary petition in bankruptcy or a voluntary petition for an arrangement or reorganization under the federal Bankruptcy Code;

iii.    If not removed, within sixty (60) days, the appointment of a receiver or trustee for all or substantially all of a Shareholder's property;

iv.     The entry of a final judgment, order or decree of a court of competent jurisdiction adjudicating a Shareholder to be bankrupt, and the expiration without appeal of the period, if any, allowed by a applicable law in which to appeal therefrom; or

v.      The transfer or disposition of Shares under judicial order, legal process, divorce decree or agreement, execution or attachment, other than transfer expressly provided for by another Section of this Agreement.

7.      **Intrafamily Transfers**. Notwithstanding the foregoing, upon the terms and conditions as a Shareholder shall choose, such Shareholder may voluntarily give or voluntarily offer and sell his or her Shares, or any portion thereof, to or for the benefit of such Shareholder's spouse, child or children, all without first offering such Shares in accordance with Section 3 of this Agreement; provided, however, that for any such transfer to be valid, the transferee must acknowledge and agree in writing to be bound by the terms, conditions and restrictions of this Agreement.

8.      **Closing of Purchase**. The closing of the purchase of any Shares pursuant to this Agreement shall occur at the time and place in [county] County, [state], designated by the Secretary of the Corporation by written notice of the purchaser or purchasers of the Shares, which date shall not be more than thirty (30) days subsequent to the expiration of the last option pursuant to Section 3 of this Agreement

or other applicable period of time designated in this Agreement. At such closing, the Selling Shareholder shall deliver to the purchaser or purchasers certificates representing the Shares being sold, and the purchaser or purchasers shall deliver to the Selling Shareholder by bank certified or cashier's check the purchase price therefor.

9. **Failure to Deliver Shares**. In the Event that a Shareholder or such Shareholder's legal representative or transferee becomes obligated to sell such Shareholder's Shares hereunder, but such Shareholder (hereinafter, the "Defaulting Shareholder") fails to tender such Defaulting Shareholder's Shares with the certificates duly endorsed for transfer (or in a manner otherwise acceptable to the Corporation), the purchase or purchasers of such Shares shall have, in addition to any other remedies such purchaser or purchasers may have, the option to place in escrow with any clearinghouse bank in [city], [state], an amount of cash equal to the purchase price of the Shares, to be held in escrow for the Defaulting Shareholder or for the heirs, devisees, executors, administrators, personal representatives, spouse, successors, or assigns, as the case may be, of the Defaulting Shareholder. The purchaser or purchasers shall then have the authority to cause to be cancelled such certificate or certificates and otherwise to cause the Corporation to treat such Shares as having been purchased by the purchaser or purchasers. Furthermore, all rights of the Defaulting Shareholder or such Defaulting Shareholder's legal representative or transferee in and to the Defaulting Shareholder's Shares shall then terminate. The Corporation shall give written notice of the Defaulting Shareholder of any invocation of this Section 9. The escrowed cash shall be released to the Defaulting Shareholder by the clearinghouse bank only upon proof satisfactory to said bank of the destruction or loss of the certificate or certificates representing such Shares.

10. **Equitable Remedies**. In the event of any actual or threatened default in or breach of any of the terms, conditions and provisions of this Agreement, the party or parties who are thereby aggrieved shall have, in addition to any and all other rights and remedies at law or in equity, the right to specific performance or injunctive relief, and all such rights and remedies shall be cumulative.

11.     **Legend**. The Share certificates evidencing the Shares shall bear, in addition to any other appropriate legends, the following legend:

> The shares represented by this
> certificate are subject to and
> transferable only in accordance with
> that certain Shareholders' Agreement by
> and among the Corporation and its
> Shareholders dated as of [effective
> date], together with amendments and
> addenda thereto, if any. Upon the
> written request to the Corporation at its
> principal place of business, a copy of
> such Agreement will be furnished
> without charge to the holder of this
> certificate.

12.     **Voting of Shares**. The Shareholders hereby agree to vote their Shares in a manner to cause the Majority Shareholder or the Majority Shareholder's designee to be elected as the sole member of the Board of Directors of the Corporation. Such designee shall be designated by the Majority Shareholder by notice to all Shareholders at least ten (10) days prior to any Shareholders' meeting called to elect directors. In the absence of such designation, the Majority Shareholder shall be elected as the sole director.

13.     **Arbitration**. In the event of any dispute arising between the parties concerning this Agreement or its interpretation, the same shall be resolved by submission to arbitration pursuant to the Commercial Arbitration Rules of the American Arbitration Association (hereinafter, the "AAA") in [city], [state], or any other mutually convenient location on which the parties may agree. Upon ten (10) days' notice to the other parties, any party may demand arbitration. Within ten (10) days after the receipt of such demand for arbitration, the parties shall each select one (1) arbitrator and shall notify the other party in writing of the person so selected. Within ten (10) days after their selection, the arbitrators so selected shall name a third arbitrator.

Together the three (3) persons so named shall constitute the arbitrators to make the determination as herein provided.

In the event any party shall fail to select an arbitrator with the time provided, or in the event the two (2) initially selected arbitrators are unable to agree on the selection of the third arbitrator, within five (5) days after any such failure or inability to name an arbitrator, the named arbitrator or arbitrators, as the case may be, may request the AAA, under its rules then obtaining, to designate such third arbitrator.

Any award made by such arbitrators shall be binding and conclusive for all purposes hereof. Such award may include injunctive relief and may be entered as a final judgment in any court of competent jurisdiction. The costs and expenses of such arbitration shall be born in accordance with the determination of the arbitrators.

14.    **Consent of Spouses**. Regardless of whether a spouse, if any, of a Shareholder obtains any community interest in the Shares or future shares, each Spousal Consent attached to this Agreement shall nevertheless apply to and bind any such spouse, the Shares, or any interest therein, and no execution by a married Shareholder of this Agreement shall be effective without the signature of such Shareholder's spouse.

In the event that any Shareholder who may divorce should subsequently remarry, such Shareholder shall either (i) cause his or her prospective spouse to execute a prenuptial agreement that shall provide that such spouse shall have no interest whatsoever in the Shareholder's Shares or (ii) request such prospective spouse to execute such documents as the Corporation may deem necessary to evidence the consent and agreement of such prospective spouse to the provisions of this Agreement and to its binding effect upon community property interest, if any, that such prospective spouse may then or thereafter own.

The agreement by any current or future spouse of a Shareholder that the termination of a marital relationship with such Shareholder for any reason shall not have the effect of removing any

Shares otherwise subject to this Agreement from the provisions of this Agreement.

15.     **Consent of the Corporation**. The Corporation hereby consents to the terms and provision of this Agreement and agrees to register the transfer of its Common Stock only in accordance herewith.

16.     **Deposit of Agreement**. The Corporation shall cause an executed counterpart of this Agreement to be inserted into its corporate minute book and shall cause its share transfer records to be marked to indicate the transfer of the Shares is restricted in accordance with the terms and provisions of this Agreement.

17.     **Termination**. This Agreement shall terminate automatically upon (i) the bankruptcy or dissolution or the Corporation or (ii) the concurrent sale of all of the Shares subject to this Agreement or (iii) an instrument in writing executed by all of the then current Shareholders and their respective transferees.

18.     **Integration**. This Agreement represents the entire understanding and agreement among the parties hereto with respect to the subject matter hereof. All prior negotiations, understandings and agreements, whether verbal or written, among the parties hereto relating to the subject matter hereof are hereby superseded.

19.     **Benefit**. This Agreement shall be binding upon, and inure to the benefit of, the parties hereto and each party's heirs, devisees, executors, administrators and personal representatives and, to the extent permitted herein, the successors and assigns of each party.

20.     **Amendment**. Unless an amendment, modification or alteration of this Agreement be in writing and be signed by each then-current Shareholder and (if applicable) the spouse of each then-current Shareholder, no amendment, modification or alternation hereof shall be valid and effective.

21.     **Notice**. Any notice required or permitted hereunder shall be deemed sufficiently given if (i) in writing and (ii) either

personally delivered or sent by certified mail, postage prepaid, addressed to the party at the address set forth below, or at such other address as the part may subsequently designated in writing, with a copy to any legal counsel that shall be designated by the party.

If to the Corporation:     [name and address]

If to the Majority Shareholder:  [name and address]

with a copy to [counsel's name and address]

If to the Minority Shareholder:  [name and address]

with a copy to [counsel's name and address]

22.  **Waiver**. The waiver of any provisions hereof shall be effective only if in writing and signed by the parties hereto, and then only in the specific instance and for the particular purposes for which such waiver is given. No failure to exercise, and no delay in exercising, any right or remedy hereunder, nor any single or partial exercise of such right or remedy, nor any exercise of any other right or remedy, operate as a waiver of any right or remedy under this Agreement.

23.  **Counterparts**. This Agreement may be executed in one (1) or more counterparts, each of which shall be deemed any original and all of which, when taken together, shall constitute the same instrument. Notwithstanding that all of the parties may not have executed the same counterpart or counterparts, upon the execution by any party of any counterpart to this Agreement, the Agreement shall be valid and binding on such party.

24.  **Headings**. Section headings used herein are inserted for convenience of description only, are not part of this Agreement, and are not to affect the construction of this Agreement.

25.  **Governing Law**. This Agreement shall be construed in accordance with, and governed by, the laws of the State of [state] as amended from time to time.

26.     **Construction**. Each party acknowledges that he or she has had the opportunity to (i) review and revise this Agreement and (ii) to present this Agreement to his or her legal counsel for advice. The parties further agree that the normal rule of construction to the effect that any ambiguities are to be resolved against the drafting party shall not be employed in the interpretation of this Agreement or any amendments or exhibits thereto.

27.     **Pronouns**. All pronouns used in this Agreement shall be deemed to include the singular or plural, or the masculine or feminine or neuter, as necessary or appropriate to effect the intent of this Agreement.

IN WITNESS WHEREOF, the parties have duly executed this Agreement on the dates shown below to be effective as of [effective date].


SHAREHOLDERS:


_____
[Name of Majority Shareholder]


_____
[Name of Minority Shareholder]


CORPORATION:

[Name of Corporation]
A [state] Corporation

By:     _____
        [Name], President

## SPOUSAL CONSENT OF [NAME]

I, the spouse of [name of Shareholder], do hereby consent and agree to the provisions of this Agreement and its binding effect upon community property interest, if any, that I may now or hereafter own. I agree that a termination of my marital relationship with [name of Shareholder] for any reason shall not have the effect of removing any Shares otherwise subject to this Agreement from the provisions hereof and that my knowledge, understanding, consent and agreement are evidenced by my execution of this consent.

I further agree that upon the award of any of the Shares to me or for my benefit pursuant to a court order or final judgment entered in any cause of action, or the allocation of any Shares to me or for my benefit pursuant to the terms of a settlement agreement entered into as part of the dissolution of my marital relationship with [name of Shareholder], all of the Shares so awarded or allocated shall be deemed to be offered to [name of Shareholder] for cash at the net book value thereof, as determined in accordance with generally accepted accounting principles by the certified public accountants regularly retained to compile the books and records of the Corporation.

I further agree that [name of Shareholder] shall have a period of sixty (60) days from the date of any such award or allocation to accept such offer, which offer may be accepted by the delivery of written notice thereof to me at the address of the Corporation, or at any address I may in future designate, within the applicable time period. In the event [name of Shareholder] does not accept such offer within said sixty-day (60-day) period, then the Shares so awarded or allocated shall be deemed to be offered to the other Shareholders, *pro rata* or in such other proportion as they may agree. Such other Shareholders shall have a period of one hundred twenty (120) days from the date of any such award or allocation to accept such offer in the manner stated above. The closing of the purchase of such Shares shall occur in accordance with the provisions of Section 8 of this Agreement.

I agree that in the event that any Shares remain after the exercise of options by [name of Shareholder] and the other Shareholders, such

Shares may be transferred in accordance with such award or allocation; provided, however, that such Shares remain subject to the restrictions set forth in this Agreement.

I understand that my consent to this Agreement in no way deems me to be a Shareholder of the Corporation.

I confirm that I am aware that my spouse, [name of Shareholder], is freely entering into this Agreement, that I have had opportunity to read this Agreement in its entirety, that I have had the opportunity to ask and have answered questions concerning this Agreement, and that I have had the opportunity to seek advice from separate legal counsel concerning the effect, if any, this Agreement would have on my future financial security should my marital relationship terminate.

IN WITNESS WHEREOF, I have executed this Consent on the date shown below to be effective [effective date].

Date: _____        _____

[Name of Spouse of Shareholder]

## FORM OF ADDENDUM FOR FUTURE SHAREHOLDER

It is my wish to purchase _____ (_____) shares of the common stock, par value $0.01 per share, of [name of corporation], a [state] corporation.

I fully understand that such shares are subject to the restrictions set forth in that certain Shareholders' Agreement dated [effective date], between the Corporation and its Shareholders (the "Shareholders' Agreement").

As a condition to purchase of shares, I am prepared to execute this Addendum accepting the terms and conditions of the Shareholders' Agreement.

____ I am not married.

or

____ Contemporaneously with my execution of this Addendum, my spouse is executing a consent in the form attached hereto.


Date: _____          _____
                          [Name of Future Shareholder]

## FORM OF SPOUSAL CONSENT
## OF SPOUSE OF FUTURE SHAREHOLDER

I, the spouse of [name of Future Shareholder], do hereby consent and agree to the provisions of this Agreement and its binding effect upon community property interest, if any, that I may now or hereafter own. I agree that a termination of my marital relationship with [name of Future Shareholder] for any reason shall not have the effect of removing any Shares otherwise subject to this Agreement from the provisions hereof and that my knowledge, understanding, consent and agreement are evidenced by my execution of this consent.

I further agree that upon the award of any of the Shares to me or for my benefit pursuant to a court order or final judgment entered in any cause of action, or the allocation of any Shares to me or for my benefit pursuant to the terms of a settlement agreement entered into as part of the dissolution of my marital relationship with [name of Future Shareholder], all of the Shares so awarded or allocated shall be deemed to be offered to [name of Future Shareholder] for cash at the net book value thereof, as determined in accordance with generally accepted accounting principles by the certified public accountants regularly retained to compile the books and records of the Corporation.

I further agree that [name of Future Shareholder] shall have a period of sixty (60) days from the date of any such award or allocation to accept such offer, which offer may be accepted by the delivery of written notice thereof to me at the address of the Corporation, or at any address I may in future designate, within the applicable time period. In the event [name of Future Shareholder] does not accept such offer within said sixty-day (60-day) period, then the Shares so awarded or allocated shall be deemed to be offered to the other Shareholders, *pro rata* or in such other proportion as they may agree. Such other Shareholders shall have a period of one hundred twenty (120) days from the date of any such award or allocation to accept such offer in the manner stated above. The closing of the purchase of such Shares shall occur in accordance with the provisions of Section 8 of this Agreement.

I agree that in the event that any Shares remain after the exercise of options by [name of Future Shareholder] and the other Shareholders, such Shares may be transferred in accordance with such award or allocation; provided, however, that such Shares remain subject to the restrictions set forth in this Agreement.

I understand that my consent to this Agreement in no way deems me to be a Shareholder of the Corporation.

I confirm that I am aware that my spouse, [name of Future Shareholder], is freely entering into this Agreement, that I have had opportunity to read this Agreement in its entirety, that I have had the opportunity to ask and have answered questions concerning this Agreement, and that I have had the opportunity to seek advice from separate legal counsel concerning the effect, if any, this Agreement would have on my future financial security should my marital relationship terminate.

IN WITNESS WHEREOF, I have executed this Consent on the date shown below to be effective [effective date].

Date: _____

_____

[Name of Spouse of Future Shareholder]

# SAMPLE ASSIGNMENT
# OF SHARES

For good and adequate consideration, the receipt of which is hereby acknowledged, I, [name of assignor] (the Assignor), do hereby assign my ownership, together with all rights and privileges thereto, in [number of shares expressed in words] (number of shares expressed in digits) shares of the [common/preferred] shares (the Shares) of [name of corporation], a [state] corporation (Corporation) to [name of assignee] (Assignee).

Such Shares are represented by share certificate(s) number [number of certificate(s)] representing [number expressed in words] (number expressed in digits) Shares. I understand that such certificate, which is attached hereto, or in the absence of which I have given an affidavit of lost certificate, will be cancelled in the share records by an authorized representative of the Corporation and a new share certificate issued to Assignee. I hereby authorize and direct any authorized representative of the Corporation to transfer the Shares on the share records of the Corporation.

_____

Effective Date

_____

Signature of Assignor

_____

Typed or Printed Name of Assignor

---

# SAMPLE ARTICLES OF MERGER

---

This sample is not intended for specific use. Each state has different requirements and different language concerning what must be included in a plan of merger and articles of merger. If each of the merging entities was formed in a different state, the articles must be filed in each state and conform to the statutes of each state. An attorney should be consulted.

This sample is based on the premise that two corporations are merging. The survivor is incorporated in one state, and the merged corporation is incorporated in another state.

## ARTICLES OF MERGER OF
## [NAME OF MERGED CORPORATION]
## INTO [SURVIVING CORPORATION]

Pursuant to the provisions of [statute] and [statute], the undersigned corporations, one of which is a [first state] corporation and one of which is a [second state] corporation, do hereby adopt the following Articles of Merger for the purposes of merging into one corporation.

## ARTICLE FIRST

The Plan of Merger that was adopted in accordance with [controlling statute of the first state] and [controlling statute of the second state] providing for the merger of [name of merged corporation], a [state] corporation (the "Merged Corporation"), into [name of surviving corporation], a [state] corporation (the "Surviving Corporation"), is attached hereto as Exhibit A.

## ARTICLE SECOND

The names of the undersigned corporations and the laws of the state under which such corporations were formed are:

| Name of Corporation | State |
| --- | --- |
| [Surviving Corporation] | [Name of Its State] |
| [Merged Corporation] | [Name of Its State] |

## ARTICLE THIRD

As to each of the undersigned corporations, the approval of whose shareholders is required, the number of shares outstanding, all of which are designated as common stock and entitled to vote on such Plan of Merger, are as follows:

| Name of Corporation | Number of Shares Outstanding and Entitled to Vote |
| --- | --- |
| [Surviving Corporation] | [Number of Shares] |
| [Merged Corporation] | [Number of Shares] |

## ARTICLE FOURTH

As to each of the undersigned corporations, the approval of whose shareholders is required, the holders of all shares outstanding and entitled to vote have signed a consent in writing approving said Plan of Merger pursuant to [statute of first state] and [statute of second state].

or

As to each of the undersigned corporations, the approval of whose shareholders is required, the number of shares voted for and against the Plan of Merger, respectively, are as follows:

| Name of Corporation | Shares Voted For | Shares Voted Against |
|---|---|---|
| [Surviving Corporation] [Merged Corporation] | [Number of Shares] | [Number of Shares] |

## ARTICLE FIFTH

The Plan of Merger and the performance of its terms were duly authorized by all action required by the laws of the States of [first state] and [second state] and by their constituent documents.

## ARTICLE SIXTH

The Surviving Corporation hereby (a) appoints the Secretary of State of [state of Merged Corporation] its agent to accept service of process in a proceeding to enforce any obligation or the rights of dissenting shareholders of each corporation that is a party to this merger; and (b) agrees that it will promptly pay to the dissenting shareholders of each corporation that is a party to this merger the amount, if any, to which they are entitled under [statute] and [statute].

## ARTICLE SEVENTH

The street address of the registered office or the principal office of the Surviving Corporation in the State of [state of Merged Corporation] to which the Secretary of State of [state of Merged Corporation] may mail service of process is [address of registered office in state of Surviving Corporation].

## ARTICLE EIGHTH

The merger will become effective on the date the Articles of Merger are filed with the Secretary of State of [state of Surviving Corporation].

or

The merger will become effective on [specific date].

[SURVIVING CORPORATION]
A [State] Corporation

By: _____
       Name: _____
       Title: _____

[MERGED CORPORATION]
A [State] Corporation

By: _____
       Name: _____
       Title: _____

# SAMPLE ARTICLES
# OF CONVERSION

This sample is not intended for specific use. Each state has different requirements regarding information that must be included in articles converting one entity to another. Consult the statutes of your state.

ARTICLES OF CONVERSION
OF
[NAME OF CORPORATION]
(the "Converting Entity")
TO
[NAME OF LIMITED LIABILITY COMPANY]
(the "Converted Entity")

Article One.

The Converting Entity is [name], a corporation formed under the laws of the state of [State].

Article Two.

The Converting Entity has approved a plan of conversion (the "Plan").

Article Three.

The Plan has been duly executed and is on file at the Converting Entity's principal place of business at [address]. A duly executed copy of the Plan will be on file, from and after the conversion, at the principal place of business of the Converting Entity at [address].

Article Four.

A copy of the Plan will be furnished by the Converting Entity (prior to the conversion) or the Converted Entity (after the conversion), on written request and without cost, to any shareholder of the Converting Entity or any member of the Converted Entity.

### Article Five.

The Converting Entity has [number in words] (number in digits) shares of common stock, no par value, issued and outstanding. No shares of any class or series are entitled to vote as a class.

All of the shares of the Converting Entity voted in favor of adopting the Plan, and no shares of the Converting Entity voted against adopting the Plan.

### Article Six.

The Converted Entity will be liable for the payment of all duly owed fees and franchise taxes, if any, that have not been paid by the Converting Entity in connection with the conversion.

*Signature of Officer*
[Name], [Office Held]

# SAMPLE ARTICLES OF ORGANIZATION OF A LIMITED LIABILITY COMPANY

This sample is not intended for specific use. Each state has different requirements and different language concerning what must be included in articles of organization. Consult your state's statutes.

## ARTICLES OF ORGANIZATION
## OF
## [NAME OF COMPANY]

A [State] Limited Liability Company

The undersigned, a natural person of the age of eighteen (18) years or more, acting as an organizer of a limited liability company (the "Company") under the [enabling statute] (the "Act"), hereby adopts the following Articles of Organization for such limited liability company:

### ARTICLE I - NAME

The name of the Company is [name].

### ARTICLE II - DURATION

The period of its duration is [number] years from the date on which these articles are filed by the [State] Secretary of State.

or

The Company shall have perpetual duration.

## ARTICLE III - PURPOSE

The purpose for which the Company is organized is the transaction of any or all lawful business for which limited liability companies may be organized under the Act.

## ARTICLE IV - PRINCIPAL PLACE OF BUSINESS, REGISTERED OFFICE AND REGISTERED AGENT

The street address of the Company's principal place of business in [State] is [address of principal place of business]. The street address of the Company's registered office is [address of registered office], and the name of its initial registered agent at such address is [name of registered agent].

## ARTICLE V - INITIAL MANAGERS

The Company is to be managed by a manager or managers. The name and address of each person who is to serve as a manager until the first annual meeting of members or until that manager's successor is duly elected are [name and address of each initial manager].

or, if the company is to be managed by its members:

## ARTICLE V - MANAGEMENT BY MEMBERS

The management of the Company is reserved to its members, and the name and address of each member are [name and address of each initial member].

## ARTICLE VI - ORGANIZER

The name and address of the organizer are [name and address of organizer].

---

[Name], Organizer

# COMPARISON OF LLC
# TO A PARTNERSHIP

The LLC actually resembles a partnership more than it does a corporation. Unlike the general partners in a partnership, all of the participants in the LLC are insulated from personal liability.

| CHARACTERISTIC | LLC | PARTNERSHIP |
|---|---|---|
| NUMBER OF OWNERS | no limit | at least two |
| TYPE OF OWNERS | no restrictions | no restrictions, except as to general partners of a limited partnership |
| CLASSES OF OWNERS | unlimited flexibility | unlimited flexibility |
| MANAGEMENT | members or managers | partners, except in limited partnership only general partners |
| TRANSFER OF INTERESTS | restrictions | restrictions |
| DURATION | perpetual, with events triggering dissolution | perpetual, with events triggering dissolution |
| LIMITED LIABILITY | all members, managers, and officers | limited partners only, except in registered limited liability partnership all the partners for certain covered acts |
| TAXATION | full pass-through, but franchise taxes may apply | full pass-through, but state may assess franchise taxes |

# COMPARISON OF LLC TO S AND C CORPORATIONS

The primary reason the LLC is chosen over the corporate form is to avoid personal liability while enjoying full pass-through status for federal taxation. S corporations enjoy the same tax status but must meet rigorous requirements that affect the flexibility of structuring.

| CHARACTERISTIC | LLC | S CORPORATION | C CORPORATION |
|---|---|---|---|
| NUMBER OF OWNERS | no limit | no more than 75 | no limit |
| TYPE OF OWNERS | no restriction | no for-profit corporations no nonresident aliens no partnerships, no LLCs only certain trusts, pension plans | any individual or person |
| CLASSES OF OWNERS | unlimited flexibility in regulations | one class | unlimited flexibility in articles, but amendments must be formally filed to reflect changes thereto |
| MANAGEMENT | members or managers | centralized | centralized |
| TRANSFERABILITY OF INTERESTS | unanimous consent | restrictive, due to 75-shareholder limitation | free transferability |
| DURATION | may be perpetual | may be perpetual | may be perpetual |
| TAXATION | may choose on federal level, although state may specify | pass-through on federal level – varies by state specifications | double taxation |

# L

punitive damages, 9

# Q

quality of work product, 155
quorum
    defined, 95
    majority of directors at meeting,
      104

# R

ratification, 20
registered agent, 6, 75, 140
    limited liability company, 131
registered limited liability partnership,
    23, 49, 50
    defined, 49
    formation, 50
    liability insurance, 51
    name, 50
    operation, 51
    termination, 52
registered office, 75, 140
    limited liability company, 131
regulations, 25
    limited liability company, 129
representative
    defined, 49
resolutions
    sample, 207
*respondeat superior*
    defined, 17
restated articles of incorporation, 141
reverse stock split, 140
right of alienation, 59, 89
right of first refusal, 56

# S

S corporation
    compared to limited liability
      company, 253
sale of all or substantially all of the
    assets, 139

defined, 139
generally, 143
rights of dissenters, 143
sales tax permit, 28, 29
samples
    articles of conversion, 247
    articles of incorporation, 191
      nonprofit corporation, 195
      professional corporation, 199
    articles of merger, 243
    articles of organization
      limited liability company, 249
    assignment of shares, 241
    assumed name certificate for an
      unincorporated entity, 183
    certificate of limited partnership,
      185
    minutes of telephonic meeting, 219
    officer's certificate, 217
    resolutions, 207
    shareholders' agreement, 221
    written consent in lieu of
      organizational meeting, 201
secretary of state, 6, 25, 43, 60, 61,
    65, 69, 77, 115, 116, 120, 121,
    122, 130, 139, 142
Section 351 filing, 30
Securities Act of 1933, 90, 108, 109,
    146
Securities and Exchange Act of 1934,
    108, 109
Securities and Exchange Commission,
    64, 146, 151
share certificate, 89
    effective date, 84
    restriction on transferability, 89
share subscription, 121
    defined, 100
shareholder
    liability, 98
    limited liability, 66
    rights of dissenters, 143
    risk limited to investment, 98
    taxation, 60
shareholders' agreement, 55
    provision for death or divorce, 64

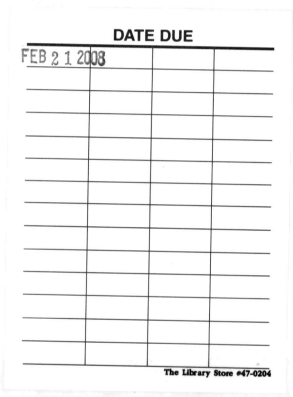